National Art Library

Japanese Art

I. Japanese Books and Albums of Prints in Colour in the National Art Library South

Kensington

National Art Library

Japanese Art
I. Japanese Books and Albums of Prints in Colour in the National Art Library South Kensington

ISBN/EAN: 9783337184018

Printed in Europe, USA, Canada, Australia, Japan

Cover: Foto ©Thomas Meinert / pixelio.de

More available books at **www.hansebooks.com**

DEPARTMENT OF SCIENCE &
ART ; OF THE COMMITTEE
OF COUNCIL ON EDUCATION

JAPANESE ART

I. JAPANESE BOOKS

AND ALBUMS OF PRINTS IN COLOUR

IN THE NATIONAL ART LIBRARY

SOUTH KENSINGTON

LONDON
Printed for Her Majesty's Stationery Office
By Eyre and Spottiswoode
Printers to the Queen's Most Excellent Majesty
1893

This Catalogue has been compiled by Mr. Edward F. Strange, an Assistant in the National Art Library, from translations kindly furnished by Mr. G. Kowaki, of the Japan Society.

Part II., dealing with Original Drawings, Prints, Stencils, Photographs of Works of Art, and Works in the Library relating to Japanese Art generally, is in preparation and will be issued shortly.

W. H. JAMES WEALE.

Itsukushima was formerly Itsukishima.

01·E·1.   History & Legend

03·G·1.   Historical & Legendary characters.

03·G·2   "   .   "

01·A·25   "   "   "

01·A·26   "   "   "

01·B·5   "   "   "

01·B·6   "   "   "

01·B·23   "   "   "

02·B·26   "   "   "

版 = Printer when with a name.
    Han or Pan
    Hankō = printer (block)
    Shuppan = printed matter.
         now

NOTICE

The present Catalogue has been undertaken for the purpose of rendering the large collection of Japanese Books, Prints, and Drawings in the National Art Library more easily accessible to Artists, Designers, and Students.

With this view, although the books are catalogued when possible, under names of authors, a subject classification has been adopted, which is based solely on the character of the illustrations; and titles are repeated in as many sections as seemed necessary.

For the same reason, in addition to the Japanese name (often a fanciful one) of a work, a descriptive title in English is given in every case, the nature of the illustrations is specified, and the size of the book or plate, shown in inches.

The collection includes a large number of Albums of Xylographic Prints in Colour; the classification of Albums which has been somewhat difficult, by reason of the variety of subjects generally found in each. The plan adopted has been that of placing each volume according to the class of subject which predominates therein.

In addition to the short titles printed in this Catalogue, each Album contains, in manuscript, an amplified description; an Index to the names of the different Artists represented, with references to their work; and (since many of the plates are incomplete) an account of whatever deficiencies may exist.

In requisitioning works mentioned herein, the press-mark only should be quoted.

E. F. S.

CONTENTS

Lacquer   IV d.

Leather.   IV d.

CLASS-INDEX

BAIREI,Kono.- Bairei Gwafu. Pictures of Birds,Insects, etc. cuts.col. vols.1,3 of a set of 3 (7x5) Kyoto 1887. 04.D.17.
BAIREI,Kono.- Bairei Kiku Hiaku-shu. The Hundred Chrysanthemums. cuts. col. vols.1,2 of 3 ($9\frac{3}{4}$x$6\frac{1}{2}$) Tokyo, Meiji24,25 (A.D. 1891-92) 08.8.13.

A LIST OF
JAPANESE BOOKS
AND
ALBUMS OF PRINTS IN COLOUR
IN THE
NATIONAL ART LIBRARY.

SECTION I.—ANIMALS AND PLANTS.

(BOOKS, ETC., CONTAINING ILLUSTRATIONS OF ANIMAL- AND PLANT-FORM.)

ANIMALS.—Yehon Shoshin Hashiradate. Illustrations of Animals, Flowers, etc. *Cuts.* 3 vols. (10 × 7) Kyōto, 1761. **O3. C. 1.**

AWOYE, H.—Tobacco Culture at Osumi and Satsuma. Text in Japanese, with an introduction, and descriptions of the illustrations in English. *Cuts, col. by hand.* (10 × 6) Tōkyō, 1878. **O3. F. 15.**

BAIREI, Kōno.—Bairei Hyakuchō Gwafu. The Hundred Birds. *Cuts, col.* 3 vols. (10 × 7) Tōkyō, 1881. Bairei died in 1895. **O3. C. 2.**

The original Drawings made for this work are in the National Art Library; and several of the Wood Blocks are exhibited in the Museum.

Second Series. *Cuts, col.* 3 vols. (10 × 7) Tōkyō, 1884. **O3. F. 14.**

———— Inaka-no-Tsuki. Birds, Animals, and Fishes, with Plants and Trees. *Cuts, col.* Vol. 1 of a set of 3. (10 × 7) Kyōto, 1889. **O3. C. 3.**

BIRDS.—Somoku Kwachō Zufu. Pictures of Birds, Flowers, etc. *Cuts, col.* (7 × 7). **O4. C. 1.**

———— Studies of Bird-form. *Cuts, tinted.* (5 × 8). **O4. D. 1.**

BIRDS.—Yehon Tekagami. Birds and Plants. *Cuts.* (9 × 6).
O3. E. 1.

BUMMEI, BUNKŌ, GEPPŌ, etc.—Pictures (17) of Birds, Fishes, Flowers, etc. *Cuts, col.* (8¾ × 13¼).
O3. D. 1.

BUNREI.—Bunrei Gwasen. Selected sketches of Birds, Plants, etc. Vols. 1 (and 2) by Bunrei, vol. 3 by his pupils. *Cuts.* Vols. 1, 3, of a set of 3. (11 × 7) Yedo, 1778.
O3. B. 1.

BUNREI, Mayekawa.—Bunrei Gwafu. Studies of Birds and Plants. *Cuts, col.* 2 vols. (14 × 10) Kyōto, 1885.
O4. F. 1.

FISHES.—Illustrations of Fishes and Insects. Vols. 14 and 15 of a set, bound in 1. *Cuts.* (10 × 8).
O3. B. 2.

FLOWERS.—Sōmoku Kwachō Zuye. Pictures of Birds and Flowers. *Cuts, col.* (7 × 5).
O4. C. 2.

GYOKURANSAI.—Banshō Shashin Zufu. Plants, Birds, etc. *Cuts, col.* (7 × 5).
O4. C. 3.

HENYEI.—Gentai Gwafu. Text book of Views, Trees, Figures, Buildings, etc., from the Chinese. *Cuts.* 5 vols. (10 × 7) Yedo, 1806.
O5. B. 15.

HIROSHIGE, Ichiryūsai.—Yehon Tebiki-gusa. Primary Introduction to Pictures of Flowers and Fishes, for children. *Cuts, col.* Vol. 1 of a series. (7 × 5), 1848.
O4. C. 4.

HOKUJU.—Hokuju Gwafu. Pictures of Figures, Flowers, Views, etc.; by Hokuju, pupil of Hokusai. *Cuts, col.* (7 × 5).
O4. C. 7.

HOKUSAI.—Denshin Kaishu. Studies of various subjects. *Cuts, col.* (9 × 6) Nagoya, 1812.
O3. E. 9.

———— Hokusai Gwayen. Studies from Life, Flowers, etc. *Cuts, col.* Vols. 1, 3, of a series. (9 × 6) Yedo, 1843.
O3. E. 11.

———— Hokusai Mangwa. Collection of Sketches. *Cuts, col.* 14 vols. (2 copies of vol. 5, 1 with extra cuts). (9 × 6), 1834.
O3. E. 8.

———— Santai Gwafu. Three Styles of painting Figures, Fishes, Birds, etc. *Cuts, col.* (9 × 6), Nagoya.
O3. E. 12.

OKUSAI,(Katsushika Taito)- Kwachō Gwaden, Ill.of
    Flowers,Birds. cuts.col. 2 vols. (9x6) Yedo &
    Ōsaka n.d. Reprint of 1848-49 ed.   05.A.30.
OKUSAI (Katsushika)- Kwachō Gwaden. Ill. of
    Flowers & Birds. cuts.col. 2 vols. (9x6) Tōkyō
    1891. repro. of orig. ed. cuts redrawn. 05.A.22.
OKUSAI,Katsushika.- Kwachō Gwafu. Ill. of
    Flowers & Birds. cuts. col. vol.1 of 2.
    (8½x6) Tōkyō, Ka-ei 1. (A.D. 1848)   08.C.4.
OKUSAI,(School of) - Kioka hyaku Kwachō. A
    Hundred Humorous poems on Flowers & Birds. Ill.
    by the Katsushika club. cuts.col, vol.1 of a
    series. (9¼x6½)   08.B.16.
    This club would have been composed of pupils &
    admirers of Hokusai.

HOKUSAI.—Kwachō Gwafu. Sketches of flowers and birds; from the originals of Hokusai by Murakoshi Riōzō; engraved by Yamada Yeinosuke. *Cuts, col.* (10 × 7) Tōkyō, 1890. *05.F.16* ~~03.F.23~~

KASHU, Numada.- Shucho Gwafu. Pictorial Monograph of Birds. cuts.col. vol.1 of a set. (10x7) Tokyo 1885. 05.A.24.
KUATEI.Taki.- A collection of Flowers & Birds. 2pp. 12 colour-prints. (9x14) Tokyo 1887. 04.F.14.

KEINEN, Imao.—Keinen Kwachō Gwafu. Birds and flowers (arranged according to the four Seasons). Engraved by Tanaka Jirokichi; printed by Miki Nisaburō. *Cuts, col.* 4 vols. (15 × 10) Kyōto, 1891-92. **04. B. 7.**

KEISAI (~~Ikkeisai~~).—Giobai Riaku Gwashiki. Rough sketches of fish and shells. *Cuts, col.* (10 × 7) (~~1810~~). **05. C. 11.**
Kitao Masayoshi) Bunkwa 10= 1813
KIOSAI. Kawanabe.- Yehon takakagami. (Ill. Mirror of Hawks) Ill. of the various kinds of hawks with hawking scenes. cuts. vol 1.pt.3 (of 3 pts.) & vol.2 in 2 pts. (9x6) Tokyo.n.d. 05.A.29.
KWŌRIN.—Kwōrin Hiakuzu. The Hundred Designs by Kwōrin. Copied by Hōitsu, and published in memory of Kwōrin on the 100th anniversary of his death. *Cuts.* 2 vols. (10 × 7) Yedo, 1815 (Bunkwa 12th, 6th month, 2nd day). **05. F. 13.**

Date T.M. is said to have lived 1670-1748. Paris 1894 sale of Collection B.

MORIKUNI, Kōsoken Tachibana.—Yehon Ōshukubai. Pictures of noted Personages, Birds, and Flowers; Drawing Lessons in styles of various artists, etc. *Cuts.* Vols. 2-7 of a set of 7. (9 × 6) Naniwa (Ōsaka), 1740. **03. D. 2.**

———— Tōdo Kummō Zui. Encyclopædia of Chinese Natural History and Botany. *Cuts.* Vols. 11 and 13 of a set of 15. (9 × 6) Kyōto, 1624. **03. E. 4.**

14

HOKUSAI.—Ippitsu Gwafu. Rough Sketches of Men and Women, Birds, etc., copied from Fukuzensai. *Cuts, col.* (9 × 6) Nagoya. **O3. E. 14.**

IINUMA, Nagayori, Yokusai.—Shiutei Sōmoku Zusetsu. Encyclopædia of Botany—Plants. 2ed., revised by Y. Tanaka and M. Ono. *Cuts, some col.* 20 vols., and Index in English and Japanese. (11 × 7; index, 8 × 6), 1874. **O3. B. 3.**

ITŌ, Keisuke, and KAKU, Hika.—Figures and descriptions of Plants in Koishikawa Botanical Garden; by Keisuke Itō, assisted by Hika Kaku. Translated and revised from Japanese by Jinzo Matsumura. *Col. plates.* 2 vols. (17 × 11) Tōkyō, 1883. **O2. E. 2.**

not Keisen

KEISAI.—Chōjū Ryaku-gwashiki. Grotesque drawings of Animals, etc., by Keisai, engraved by Shumpūdō Nojiro Ryūko. *Cuts, col.* (10 × 7) Yedo, 1797. **O5. B. 23.**

Keisai Yeisen

————— Keisai Sogwa. Illustrations of Flowers, Fishes, Views, etc. *Cuts, col.* 5 vols. (9 × 6), 1839. **O3. E. 2.**

KEISAI Yeisen, Yoshinobu.—Keisai Ukiyo Gwafu. Sketches of customary Scenes of the Seasons, Insects, Birds, Plants, etc. *Cuts, col.* (9 × 6). **O3. D. 15.**

KONDŌ, Ariyoshi.—Taisei Shinshafu. Illustrations of Flowers, Birds, Fishes, Animals and Insects. By Kondō Ariyoshi (pupil of Ganku and lived c. 1834 at Kyōto). From the original pictures kept by Shibakawa of Ōsaka Revised and some drawn by Nambara Keisho, Ōsaka. *Cuts, col.* 2 vols. (12 × 8), 1888. **O5. A. 1.**

MORIKUNI, Kōsoken, Tachibana—Tōdo Kunmō Zui.—Encyclopædia of Chinese Natural History and Botany. *Cuts.* Vols. 11, 13, of a set of 15. (9 × 6) Kyōto, 1624. **O3. E. 4.**

————— Yehon Tsūhōshi. Pictures of various scenes of Trades, Amusements, Birds, Flowers, etc., with notes. Supplementary to "Shahōtai." *Cuts.* Vols. 1, 2, 6, of a set of 10. (9 × 6) Naniwa (Ōsaka), 1729. **O3. D. 25.**

————— Yehon Ōshukubai. Pictures of noted Personages, Birds, and Flowers; Drawing Lessons in styles of various artists, etc. *Cuts.* Vols. 2-7 of a set of 7. (9 × 6)

MORIKUNI, Kōsoken, Tachibana.—Yehon Shahōtai. Pictures of Animals, Birds, etc., with short description. Illustrated by Tachibana Morikuni. 2 ed. *Cuts.* Vols. 8, 9*a*, 9*b*, of a series. (9 × 6) Ōsaka, 1770. **O3. E. 3.**

NATURAL HISTORY.—Kummō Zui. Illustrated Encyclopædia of Natural History and Botany. *Cuts.* Vols. 5, 6, of a series. (9 × 6). **O3. D. 4.**

———— Kummō Zui Taisei. Encyclopædia of Natural History and Botany. Vol. 4, Nos. 14–19 bound together. *Cuts.* (9 × 6). **O3. D. 3.**

ONO, Motoyoshi.—Dokuhin Benran. Poisonous Plants; illustrated by K. Mogami. *Cuts, col.* 2 vols. (6 × 4) Tōkyō, 1882. **O4. C. 5.**

SHIGEMASA, Kitao, Kōsuisai.—Yehon Komagadake. Collection of famous Horses in Japan and China, with their owners, in various Scenes. *Cuts, col.* 3 vols. (9 × 6), 1802. **O3. E. 5.**

TAITO, Katsushika.—Kwachō Gwaden. Studies of Birds and Flowers; by Katsushika Taito. *Cuts, col.* Vols. 1, 2. (9 × 6), 1848–49. **O3. E. 6.**

TAKIZAWA, Kiyoshi.—Senryūdō Gwafu. Pictures of Birds, Flowers, Fishes, Shells, etc. *Cuts.* 2 vols. of a series. (9 × 6), 1879– **O3. D. 5.**

URAKAWA, Kinsuke, Issensai.—Yehon Hayamanabi. Illustrated lessons on Fishes, for children. *Cuts, col.* Vol. 3. (7 × 5) Naniwa, 1847. **O4. C. 6.**

YASUKUNI, Tachibana.—Yehon Noyama-gusa. Pictures of Plants and Flowers, with short descriptions; by Tachibana Yasukuni, coloured by Hasegawa Sadanobu, engraved by Tanaka Tadaharu. 2 ed. *Cuts, col.* 5 vols. (9 × 6) Ōsaka, 1883. **O3. E. 7.**

YŌNAN.—Kwa-i. Illustrations of Plants, collected from various books. Trees, 4 vols., of which vol. 3 is missing. Grass, 4 vols., of which vol. 1 is missing. *Cuts.* (11 × 8). **O5. B. 6.**

YOSHITOSHI, Ikkwaisai.—Ikkwai Mangwa. Pictures of Figures, Animals, Fishes, etc. *Cuts, col.* Vol. 1 of a set of 15. (7 × 5), 1866. **O4. C. 11.**

NISHIYAMA Ken-ichirō.—Kwanyei Gwafu. Sketches by
Kwanyei. Engraved by Mutō Inezō, printed by Nomura
Yeikichi. *Cuts, col.* (12 × 7) Ōsaka, 1886.   **O5. F. 11.**

Kwanyei is an assumed name of Nishiyama Ken-ichirō.

NOBUMITSU,Kuribara.- Kokon meiba dzui. Famous horses
of ancient & modern times. Compiled by Kuribara
Nobumitsu. cuts,col. Vol 1 of a series. (8¾x6)
Tōkyō (c.1800)   08.C.3

GAKUDŌ,Sanjin (pseud.) Seisha Shijū hachitaka Gwajō.
Pictures from life of the 48 varieties of Birds.
(English & French title,Japanese Paintings,Flowers
& Birds). (14x9) Tōkyō,1888. reprint. 04.B.8

WATANABE Seitei.—Seitei Kwachō Gwafu.   Studies of
flowers and birds; designed and printed by Watanabe
Seitei. *Cuts, col.* 3 vols. (10 × 7) Tōkyō, 1890–91.
                                   O5. C. 24.

1. ed. 1755.

SEITEI, Watanabe.—Bijutsu Sekai. Pictures of Birds and
Flowers. Engraved by Gotō Tokujirō, and printed by
Yoshida Ichimatsu. *Cuts, col.* (10 × 6) Tōkyō, 1894.
                        O5. F. 18 ~~O8. F. 22.~~

No. 25 (Jan. 1894) of Bijutsu Sekai; a monthly art journal.

TAKIZAWA,Kiyoshi.-Senryodō Gwafu. Ill. of Plants,
Flowers,Insects & Fishes by Senyrōdō (the
literary name of the artists' house.) cuts.
3 vols.(9x6) Tōkyō,1879-1881.   03.D.5.

TAKIZAWA,Kiyoshi.-Karakusa moyo hinagata. Coll. of
vine & flower patterns. engr. (3x6¼)
Tokyo,1881.   08.C.12.

Shumman (Shosado)

UTAMARO,Kitagawa:-Chūrui Gwafu. Pictorial monograph of the insect Family. Compiled by Yadoya-
no-Meshimori. Ill. by Kitagawa Utamaro. 2 vols.
(11x7) Yedo,1788._Pub. Tsuta-ya.   08.A.5.
UTAMARO,Kitagawa:-Chūrui Gwafu. Pictorial momo-
graph of Insect Life. Ill. by Utamaro with
humorous poems by various poets. Compiled by
Yadoya-no-Meshimori. cuts,col.(10x7)
Tokyo,1892.   05.F.17.

AKASHI, Chūshichi.- Dzugwa Hōkan Jimmei Shōden.
Detailed lives of (Chinese) Painters from
the Dzugwa Hōkan (valuable mirror of painting),
compiled in the 15th.C. seals.(7½x5) Ōsaka,
1893.   08.D.5.
BIJUTSU,Sekai.-The World Of Arts. Ed. by Watanabe
Seitei,engr. by Gotō Tokujiro, & printed by
Yoshida Ichimatsu. cuts,col. Parts 1-25.
Tōkyō, 1890-94.   05.F.18.

FUJIHIKO, Senzaiyen.—Itsukishima Hengaku Shukubon.
The painted tablets dedicated to, and kept at the temple
of Itsukishima, with explanatory notes. *Cuts.* Vol. 1,
part 2. (10×7).   O3. F. 17.

ALBUM.—Birds, Figures, Plants, etc.; by Bain, Bokukai, Gekkei, Gyokukō, Hōchū, Ippō, Kochō, Kyokukō Dojin, Masuyuki, Nangaku, Rankō, Ryūkwōsai, Shiken, Shō-kosai, Shōnen, Shōsadō, Shumman, Shuntō, Sosan, Tet-suzan, Tōkei, Tōya, and Unkwan. *Cuts, col., cut out and mounted.* (12 × 6½). **O5. A. 2.**

SECTION II.—PAINTING AND SCULPTURE.

(COLLECTIONS OF SKETCHES, REPRODUCTIONS OF PICTURES, ILLUSTRATIONS OF SCULPTURE, SEALS, ETC.)

AKATSUKI Kanenari.—Ningyō Zuye. Pictures of popular Heroes, forming subjects for Ornaments in the festival of the Shintō Temple Temmangū, in Ōsaka; compiled by Akatsuki Kanenari, illustrated by Matsugawa Han-zan. *Cuts.* (9 × 7), 1846. **O3. C. 4.**

BOKUSEN, Gekkwōtei.—Bokusen Sogwa. Sketches from Life, by Gekkwōtei Bokusen, pupil of Hokusai. *Cuts, col.* Vol. 1. (9 × 6) Nagoya, 1815. **O3. D. 6.**

BUMPŌ, Shunsei.—Bumpō Sogwa. Rough Sketches from Life. *Cuts, col.* (9 × 6) Nagoya, 1800. **O3. D. 7.**

———— Bumpō Kangwa. Sketches of Chinamen. *Cuts, tinted.* (9 × 6) Kyōto, 1803. **O3. D. 8.**

———— Bumpō Gwafu. Drawings from Life, Plants, etc. Engraved by Inouye Jihei. *Cuts, tinted.* Vols. 2, 3, of a series. (10 × 7), 1813. **O3. B 4.**

DRAWING.—Yehon Yamato Hiji Gwahō, Saishiki-no-Maki. Drawing and Painting Lessons. (9 × 6), 1742.

O3. D. 9.

GOSO...(TEI ?).—Goso Gwafu. Illustrations of Figures, Birds, Animals, Views, etc. *Cuts, col.* (9 × 6).

O3. D. 10.

Another copy, with 13 additional pp. substituted for 23 pp. of the above. **O3. D. 11.**

GYOKUSUISAI, Yoshikane.—Gwato Sen-yō. Drawings. *Cuts.* 3 vols. bound in 2. (11 × 7). **O3. B. 5.**

HAKUSHŪ.—Yehon Keito Sōshi. Book of Studies. *Cuts.* Vol. 1, part 1. (10 × 7), 1751. **O3. C. 6.**

———— Gwazu Hiakuchin. Book of Sketches. *Cuts.* Vol. 3 of a set of (?) 3. (10 × 7), 1884. **O3. C. 5.**

HARUNARI, Kitagawa, and MINWA, Aikawa.—Hengaku Kihan. Copies of Tablets in the temples at Kyōto. *Cuts.* Vol. 1. (10 × 7) Kyōto, 1819. **O3. B. 6.**

HIROSHIGE.—Tōkaidō Harimaze Zuye. Pictures of various subjects with reference to the Principal Posts along the Tōkaidō. *Cuts, col.* (14 × 9½). **O3. C. 7.**

HOKKEI.—Hokkei Mangwa. Illustrations of Figures, Animals, Birds, etc. *Cuts, col.* (9 × 6). **O3. D. 12.**

HOKUJU.—Hokuju Gwafu. Pictures of Figures, Flowers, Views, etc.; by Hokuju, pupil of Hokusai. *Cuts, col.* (7 × 5). **O4. C. 7.**

HOKUSAI.—Denshin Kaishu. Studies of various subjects. *Cuts, col.* (9 × 6) Nagoya, 1812. **O3. E. 9.**

———— Hokusai Mangwa. Collection of Sketches. *Cuts, col.* 14 vols. (2 copies of vol. 5, 1 with extra cuts). (9 × 6), 1834. **O3. E. 8.**

———— Hokusai Gwayen. Studies from Life, Flowers, etc. *Cuts, col.* Vols. 1, 3, of a series. (9 × 6) Yedo, 1843. **O3. E. 11.**

~~———— Hokusai Gwafu.—Pictures of Figures, Landscapes, Birds, Flowers, etc.—2 ed. *Cuts, col.* Vols. 1, 2. (2 × 6) Nagoya, 1875.~~ **O3. E. 10.**

———— Santai Gwafu. Three styles of painting Figures, Fishes, Birds, etc. *Cuts, col.* (9 × 6) Nagoya. **O3. E. 12.**

~~———— Various Scenes and Studies from Life. *Cuts, col.* (9 × 6).~~ **O3. E. 13.**

———— Ippitsu Gwafu. Rough Sketches of Men and Women, Birds, etc., copied from Fukuzensai. *Cuts, col.* (9 × 6) Nagoya. **O3. E. 14.**

IGUCHI,Bunzan.-Nihon Bijutsu Gwaka Jimmei Shoden.
Detailed Lives of all the Painters of Japan:
with critical notes. seals & signatures. 2 vols.
(7½x5) Osaka,1892.   08.D.2.

HIGUCHI,Bunzan.-Nihon Bijitsu Gwaka Jimmei Shoden.
History of all the painters of Japan. Compiled
by Higuchi Bunzan in Meiji 25 & revised by
Yubi-Kwan Shujin. seals & signatures. 4 vols.
(8½x6¼) Ōsaka,Meiji 30 (A.D.1897)   08.D.1.
HIGUCHI,Bunzan.-Nihon Meika Jimmei Shoden. Detailed
lives of famous men (of letters) in Japan.
Portraits,seals,signatures. 2 vols. (7½x5)
Ōsaka,1894.   08.D.4.
HIGUCHI,Bunzan.-Nihon Bijutsu Gwaka Jimmei Shoden.
Hoi. Supplementto the deatailed lives of all
the Painters of Japan. seals & signatures.
(7½x5) Ōsaka,1894.   08.D.3.

HOKUSAI.—Hokusai Gwafu. Pictures of Figures, Landscapes, Birds, Flowers, etc. 3 ed. *Cuts, col.* ~~Vols. 1, 2,~~
~~of a set of~~ 3½4(9 × 6) Nagoya, 1875.   O3. E. 10.
Another copy. 1 ed. Vol. 1 (part only).
                                              O3. E. 13.

O3. E. 13 is part of Vol 1. O3.E.10. 1 ed.

ITCHŌ,Hanabusa.-Itchō Gwasen. Selection from the
    Pictures executed by Hanabusa Itchō. cuts,
    col. (10x7) Yedo (before 1863)   reprint.
                                        05.A.26.
KANŌ School.-Yehon tokiwa-no-matsu. Hanging
    pictures & painted screens by artists of the
    Kanō School. cuts, vol 2 of 3 (11¾x8½) (?)
    Tokyo (mid. 18th.C.)   08.A.2.
KAWAGITA,Shinichirō.-Meikwa Zensho. seals &
    signatures of famous painters,poets,&
    authors. seals & signatures. 7 vols.(3¼x7¼)
    Kyōto,1854.   08.C.9.
KOKU-KWA.- Koku-Kwa (National Flower). A sel-
    ection of the best examples of Japanese
    Fine Art with explanatory Notes by various
    authors,repros. of famous Pictures,& ill.
    of typical specimens of Industrial Art. Ed.
    by Rokusaburō Yamamoto,& others. Plates,
    some col. & ill. in the text. (16x11)
    Tōkyō,1889.   02.E.1.
    also an ed. with some Eng. text.

KEISAI, Kitao.—Keisai Riakugwa-shiki. Sketches (some
    humorous) of various figures and illustrations of proverbs.
    Cuts, col. Vol. 3 of a set. (7 × 5) Yedo.   04. C. 28.

KIŌSAI, (Kawanabe Tōyuku).—Kiōsai Gwaden. Nai hen.
    Various styles of painting, with instructions in the art,
    genealogies of painters, etc. 2 vols. Gwai hen. Life
    of Kiōsai with illustrations of various incidents therein.
    Text by Uriu Masakazu, illustrations by Kawanabe
    Tōyuku (Kiōsai). 2 vols. Cuts, some col. (10 × 7)
    Tōkyō, 1887.   05. F. 9.

HOKUSŌ.—Yehon Zuhen Pictures of Figures, Animals, Plants, etc., by Hokusō; compiled by Hanabusa Ippō, his pupil. *Cuts.* 3 vols. (11 × 7) Ōsaka, 1751.

O3. B. 7.

ICHI-Ō, *Hōgen* Shumboku.—Yehon Tekagami. Pictures by celebrated Japanese and Chinese artists. *Cuts.* Vols. 2, 5, 6, of a set of 6, bound in 1. (10 × 7) Naniwa (Ōsaka), 1720. **O5. B. 4.**

———— Wakan Meigwayen. Pictures by noted Japanese and Chinese artists; copied by *Hōgen* Shumboku Ichi-ō, (at the age of 61). 1, Chinese artists; 2, Tosa school; 3, Sesshū school; 4, Ko-hōgen school; 5, Tan-yū school; 6, Miscellaneous artists. 1 ed. *Cuts.* 6 vols., (vol. 4, 2 copies). (11 × 7), 1749–50. **O3. B. 9.**

Reprint. 6 vols. (10 × 7), 1887. **O3. B. 10.**

———— Gwashi Kwaiyō. Pictures by noted Japanese and Chinese artists; compiled by *Hōgen* Shumboku Ichi-ō. 1, 2, Chinese artists; 3, Sesshū and Kano school; 4, Tosa school; 5, Kano school; 6, Miscellaneous artists. *Cuts.* 6 vols. (11 × 7) Ōsaka, 1751. **O3. B. 8.**

ICHI-Ō Sesshō.—Yehon Shūyō. Pictures of Figures, Birds, Flowers, etc. Engraved by Fujiye Shirobei. *Cuts.* 3 vols. (11 × 7) Ōsaka, 1751. **O3. B. 11.**

INSCRIPTIONS.—Shūko Jisshu. Abbreviated copies of antique Inscriptions on Tablets suspended from the gates of Temples. *Cuts.* 10 vols. (15 × 10). **O4. A. 3.**

———— Shūko Jisshu. Inscriptions on Monuments, Tiles, etc. *Cuts.* 13 vols. (15 × 10). **O4. A. 5.**

ISAI, Katsushika.—Isai Gwashiki. Collection of Drawings from Life for artists. *Cuts.* (9 × 6) Yedo, 1864.

O3. D. 13.

KEISAI Yeisen, Yoshinobu.—Ukiyo Gwafu. Sketches. *Cuts, col.* Vol. 2. (9 × 6) Yedo. **O3. D. 14.**

———— Keisai Ukiyo Gwafu. Sketches of customary Scenes of the Seasons, Insects, Birds, Plants, etc. *Cuts, col.* (9 × 6). **O3. D. 15.**

KŌCHŌ.—Kōchō Gwafu. Sketches. *Cuts, col.* 2 vols. (10 × 7), 1833. **O3. C. 8.**

MATORA, Ōishi, etc.—Jinji Andō. Pictures of various Scenes, famous Personages, etc., with humorous verses and notes. Vol. 1 illustrated by Ōishi Matora; vol. 2, by Utagawa Kuniyoshi, vols. 3, 5, by Keisai Yeisen; vol. 4, by Utagawa Kuninao. *Cuts, col.* Vols. 1, 3, 4, 5. (9 × 6) Nagoya, 1829–47. **O3. D. 20.**

MINWA.—Tsūshin Gwafu. Drawings from Life, of Men, Horses, etc. *Cuts.* (10 × 7) Nagoya, 1819.
O5. B. 1.

PICTURES.—Collection of Pictures. *Cuts, col.* (7 × 5).
O4. C. 8.

———— Meisū Gwafu. Copies of Landscapes, Figures, Flowers, etc., after various artists. *Cuts.* 3 vols. (10 × 7), 1809. **O3. C. 9.**

———— Shūko Jisshu. Copies of pictures by various artists. *Cuts.* (10 × 15). **O4. A. 1.**

———— Wakan Meihitsu Gwahō. Copies of Pictures by celebrated Japanese and Chinese artists. Vols. 3, 4, 6, of a set. *Cuts.* (10 × 7), 1771 (8th year of Meiwa).
O5. B. 2.

PORTRAITS.—Shūko Jisshu. Portraits; copied from Drawings and Carvings. *Cuts.* 5 vols. (15 × 10).
O4. A. 2.

RYŪYENDŌ.—Yōchi Yedehon. Handbook of Painting for Children. *Cuts.* (7 × 5) Yedo, 1832. **O4. C. 9.**

SEALS.—Shūko Jisshu. Collection of Seals of Mikado, Officials, Artists, etc. *Impressions of seals.* Vols. 1, 2, 4, of a set of 4, with 2 supplementary vols. and a Catalogue. (Ms. Index in English.) (11 × 8). **O5. A. 5.**

SETTEI, *Hōkyō* Tsukioka.—Kingyoku Gwafu. Drawings by various Japanese and Chinese artists. Copied by Tsukioka Settei. *Cuts.* 6 vols. (11 × 7), 1770.
O5. B. 3.

SHIBAKAWA, M.—Shūbi Gwakan. Copies of Pictures by celebrated artists. Compiled by M. Shibakawa, Ōsaka. Copied by Nambara Keisho. (With short Ms. biographies). *Cuts, col.* 2 vols. in case. (12 × 7), 1889.
O3. A. 1.

KWAMPO, Araki.—Kwaigwa Jō. Pictures by various
artists. Compiled by Araki Kwampo, *Cuts, col.* Vol. 1
of a series. (10 × 6) Tōkyō, 1892. **O3. F. 21.**

MORIKUNI, Kōsoken Tachibana.—Yehon Ōshukubai. Pictures of noted Personages, Birds, and Flowers; Drawing
Lessons in styles of various artists, etc. *Cuts.* Vols.
2-7 of a set of 7. (9 × 6) Naniwa (Ōsaka), 1740.
O3. D. 2.

NISHIYAMA Ken-ichirō.—Kwanyei Gwafu. Sketches by
Kwanyei. Engraved by Mutō Inezō, printed by Nomura
Yeikichi. *Cuts, col.* (12 × 7) Ōsaka, 1886. **O5. F. 11.**

Kwanyei is an assumed name of Nishiyama Ken-ichirō.

NIWA,Tokei.- Meika gwafu. Pictures by famous
painters. cuts.col. (11x7½) Owari,Nagoya
(late 18th.C.) O8.B.2.
NANTEI,Nishimura.- Nantei Gwafu. Pictures by
Nantei engr. by Inouye Jihei,printed by
Hori Kisaburo. cuts,col.(10¼x7) Kyoto,
Bunsei,yr. of the dog.(A.D.1826) O8.B.10.

SHUMBOKU, Hokio.—Wakan Meihitsu Yehon Tekagami. Pictures by celebrated artists of Japan and China; copied by Shumboku, Hokio. *Cuts.* 6 vols. (10 × 7) Ōsaka, 1720.　　　　　　　　　　　　　　**O5. F. 10.**

　　　　A reprint.

SUNEN,Minamoto.-Honcho guatohin moku. A catalogue of famous pictures with corr-. ections by Tani Buncho. (A copy from the original M.S. of about the middle of the 18th.C.) (9½x6½) M.S.　　　　　08.B.15.

TANYU,Kano,- Tanyu ringwa. Sketches from pictures by Tanyu. Selected by Kohitsu Ryoi. Pub. by Kogetsudo. cuts,col. vol.1 of 3. (12x8¼) Owari(c.A.D.1800)08·A·I.

TOSA,Hidenobu.- Meiji Soho Shoshu Butsuzo Dzui. New & enlarged ed. of the ill. coll. of Buddhist portraits of all sects. 5 vols. Engr. (9x7¼) Kyoto,1896.　　　03.A.9.

YŌSAI, Kikuchi—Kikuchi Yōsai Gwafu. Pictures by Kikuchi Yōsai; copied by Matsumoto Fuko, engraved by **Kimura** Tokutaro. *Cuts, col.* 2 vols. (11 × 7) Tòkyò, 1891.　　　　　　**O3. A. 2.**

SHIGENOBU, Yanagawa. — Yanagawa Gwajin. Pictures.
Cuts, col. (9 × 6) Nagoya. **O3. D. 16.**

SHŪZAN, *Hōgen* Mitsuoki.—Wakan Meihitsu Gwayei.
Copies of Pictures by celebrated Japanese and Chinese
artists. *Cuts.* (10 × 7), 1749 (2nd year of Kwan-yen).
O3. C. 10.

SKETCHES.—Collection of Sketches. *Cuts, col.* (8 × 6).
O4. C. 10.

TAKAGI.—Honchō Gwarin. Pictures by various celebrated
artists, copied by Takagi. *Cuts.* Vols. 1, 2, of a set of 3.
(11 × 7), 1752. **O5. B. 5.**

TOYOKUNI, Ichiyōsai.—Toshidama-fude. Sketches. *Cuts,
col.* (9 × 6) Nagoya. **O3. D. 17.**

Another copy. *Cuts.* (9 × 6) Nagoya. **O3. D. 18.**

YAMAMOTO, Rokusaburō.—Koku-kwa (National Flower).
A selection of the best examples of Japanese Fine Art,
with explanatory Notes by various authors, reprodu
tions of famous Pictures, and illustration   typical
specimens of Industrial Art. E   by Rokusaburō
Yamamoto. *Plate   and illustrations in the
text.* (16   Tōkyō, 1889- **O2. E. 1.**

YEITEI SHUJIN.—Nanka-no-yume. Remarks on the faults
of a Society of Artists,—a Dream; by Yeitei Shujin,
illustrated by Utagawa Sadahiro. *Cuts, col.* Vol. 1 of
a series. (9 × 6), 1835. **O3. D. 19.**

YOSHITOSHI, Ikkwaisai.—Ikkwai Mangwa. Pictures of
Figures, Animals, Fishes, etc. *Cuts, col.* Vol. 1 of a set
of 15. (7 × 5), 1866. **O4. C. 11.**

ALBUMS OF PRINTS IN COLOUR.

ALBUM.—Collection of miscellaneous Prints and Sketches
(some printed in relief); by Baishū, Chōsho, Gakutei,
Geppō, Gesshū, Goshichi, Gyodai, Gyokuho, Hakuhō,
Hanzan, Himemaru, Hokkei, Kaken, Kasetsu, Kisui,
Kōin, Kōyen, Kunisada, Kwanyei, Kwōitsu, Mimasu,
Nagamune, Nihō, Ōshuku, Shizan, Shunsei, Shunshō,
Shūtei, Tanchi, Tōnan, Tōshū, Toyokuni, Yeisai, and
Yūsetsusai. *71 sheets.* (9 × 12). **O5. A. 3.**

ALBUM.—Collection of miscellaneous Prints and Sketch(
(some printed in relief); by Hanzan, Hokkei, Hoku(
Keisai, Koryōsai, Kunisada (Toyokuni 2nd), Kuniyos(
Sessō, Tameichi (Hokusai), and Toyokuni. *37 shee(*
(12 × 9). **O5. A.**

———. Theatrical Scenes, Carved Figures by Hidari Ji(
gōrō, and a copy of Caricatures on a wall; by Kuniyos(
(Ichiyūsai), and Toyokuni. *42 sheets, in 3 portio(*
(14½ × 9¾). **O5. C. 2(**

SECTION III.—DESIGN AND ORNAMENT(

(COLLECTIONS OF MATERIAL FOR DESIGN, DIAPERS, CREST
AND PATTERNS OF VARIOUS KINDS).

See also Section IV.—HANDICRAFTS ; and
Section VII.—COSTUME.

COSTUMES.—Costumes. Two hundred patterns of Ladi(
Dresses. Vol. 2 of a set. (7 × 5), 1667. .
O4. C. 2(

DESIGNS.—Collection of Designs for Artists. *Cuts, c(*
(8 × 6). **O4. C. 1(**

——— Kintai Gwasō. Precious bag of Patterns for artist
Cuts, col. (9 × 6), 1828. **O3. D. 2(**

DIAPERS.—Shin Komonchō. Collection of two hundr(
and thirty-five Diaper Patterns. *Cuts, col.* (6 × 8).
O4. C. 1(

——— Shin Komonchō. Collection of three hundred an
sixteen Diaper Patterns. *Cuts, col.* (7 × 10).
O4. C. 14

FUTATSUYANAGI MABUCHI.—Chōkō Hinagata. Book c
Designs for Carvers. *Cuts.* Vol. 1 of a set. (9 × 6)
1827. **O3. E. 15**

GYOKUSUISAI, Yoshikane.—Gwazu Sen-yō. Designs fo
instruction in Drawing. *Cuts.* Vol. 2 of a set of 3
(11 × 7). **O5. B. 7**

HIROSHIGE, Ryūsai.—Shoshoku Gwatsū. Book of Design(
Cuts, col. Vols. 1–3 of a set. (7 × 5). **O4. C. 15**

Hokusai :- Banshoku zukō.
Reprint of Vols 1, 2, 3, 5.   *1835.*   03.E.17

KWŌRIN.—Kwōrin Hiakuzu. The Hundred Designs by Kwōrin. Copied by Hōitsu, and published in memory of Kwōrin on the 100th anniversary of his death. *Cuts.* 2 vols. (10 × 7) Yedo, 1815 (Bunkwa 12th, 6th month, 2nd day).   **O5. F. 13.**

KWŌRIN.—Kwōrin Hiakuzu. Kō hen (later volumes). Designs copied by Hōitsu, to supplement the former edition (05. F. 13). *Cuts.* 2 vols. (10 × 7) Yedo, 1826 (Bunsei 9th, 6th month).   **O5. F. 14.**

MATORA, Ōishi.—Jinji Andō. Designs for the decoration of lanterns. Vol. 1 by Ōishi Matora ; vol. 2 by Utagawa Kuniyoshi (Chōōrō) ; vol. 3 by Keisai (Yeisen) ; vol. 4 by Utagawa Kuninao ; vol. 5 by Keisai (Ippitsuan, Yeisen). *Cuts, col.* 5 vols. (9 × 6) Nagoya (Vol. 1, 1829 ; vol. 4, 1830 ; vol. 5, 1835).   **O3. D. 20.**

These lanterns are rectangular in shape, and mounted on poles ; they are used only in Shinto festival processions.

MANNEN,Suzuki.- Yamato Nishiki. The Brocade of Japan. Famous pictorial subjects relating to the months & seasons of the yr. cuts,col.
Vol.1 of a set of 5. (5x7) Kyoto 1888. 04.D.16.
The title is derived from a famous poem by Moto-ori Norinaga "Only when finished in Japanese colours does the brocade of the Chinese become valuable."

HOKUSAI, Gwakyō Rōjin, Katsushika Taito.—Yehon Shin Hinagata. Original Designs, Plans, and Working Drawings, for Engineers and others, by Hokusai (in his 77th year). *Cuts*. Vol. 1 of a set of 3. (9 × 6), 1836.
O3. D. 22.

———— Banshoku Zukō. Designs for Artists. *Cuts, col.* 5 vols. (9 × 6) Yedo, 1835–50.
O3. D. 23.

———— Kwachō Sansui Saigwa Zushiki. Designs for Art Metal-work. *Cuts*. Vols. 3, 4, of a set of 5. (5 × 7) Yedo, 1863–64.
O4. D. 2.

JŪCHIKUSAI.—Jūchikusai Gwafu. Designs; Birds, Flowers, etc. *Cuts, col.* (10 × 6).
O3. C. 11.

KEISAI, Kitao Masayoshi.—Shoshoku Gwakan. Materials for Design; engraved by Shumpūdō Nojiro Ryūko. *Cuts*. (10 × 7).
O5. B. 8.

KEISAI Yeisen.—Yehon Nishiki-no Fukuro. Book of Designs for Artists; illustrated by Keisai Yeisen. *Cuts, col.* (9 × 6) Ōsaka, 1828.
O3. D. 24.

KYŌZAN, Hirota.—Kodai Karakusa Moyōshū. Collection of ancient Diaper Patterns. (9 × 6) Tōkyō, 1885.
~~O3. F. 16.~~ *O3. E. 16*

KURIHARA [Nobumitsu.]—Patterns of Bridles. *Cuts, col.* (11 × 7), 1834.
O5. B. 9.

MURAKAMI, M.—Busō Kwōyeki Monchō. Collection of Diapers and Crests. *Engr.* (5 × 6). *1876*
O4. D. 3. ✶

———— Kokon Moyōshū. Manual of Design. Compiled by M. Murakami. *Engr., some col.* (5 × 6), 1883.
O4. D. 4.

NAKAJIMA Tanjirō.—Hinagata Yado-no-ume. Patterns of Ladies' Dresses. *Cuts*. Vol. 3. (10 × 7) Naniwa (Ōsaka), 1730.
O5. B. 13.

OCHIAI, Norikuni.—Book of Designs for Carpenters; by Norikuni Ochiai, engraved by Sentarō Yegawa. 2 ed. *Cuts*. Parts 2 of vol. 1; 1, 2, of vol. 2. (5 × 7), 1876 (9th year of Meiji).
O4. D. 6.

RINSHŌ.—Gunchō Gwayei. Designs. *Cuts*. Vol. 1, part 1, of a set. (11 × 7).
O5. B. 10.

o 75435.   B

18

SEKINE Kwanren.—Rokutai Jibiki. Six different styles of Japanese Characters. *Specimens of type.* (5×6) Osaka, 1883. **O4. D. 5.**

SHIMABARA, G.—Iroha Hayabiki, Monchō Daizen. Collection of Crests (alphabetically arranged), Names, Diapers, various styles of Characters, etc. compiled by G. S. after Designs in the "Genji Monogatari." *Engr.* (3×6), 1881. **O4. D. 7.**

SHŌKO RŌJIN, *pseud.*—Kokon Meibutsu Ruishū. Collection and Records of famous ~~objects~~/for the most part used in the Tea Ceremony. Compiled by Shōko Rōjin. *Cuts, some col.* 4 vols. in 18 parts. (9×6), 1787. **O3. D. 27.**

TATTO, Katsushika.—Banshoku Zukō. Designs. *Cuts, col.* Vols. 1, 2, 3, 5, of a set of (?) 6. (9×6) Osaka, 1885. *Sa Hokusai* **O3. E. 17.**

TAKIZAWA, K.—Karakusa Moyō Hinagata. Collection of Diapers and Designs. *Engr.* (3×6) Tōkyō, 1881. **O4. D. 8.**

ikuo TANAKA, K.—Iroha-biki Monchō. Collection of Crests (alphabetically arranged), Diapers, various styles of Characters, etc. compiled by K. T. after Designs in the "Genji Monogatari." *Engr.* (3×6) Tōkyō, 1881. **O4. D. 9.**

TANAKA Shōzaburō.—Yūhō Bijustu Ōyō. Designs for Fine Art work. Compiled by Tanaka Shōzaburō. *Cuts, col.* (10×7) Kyōto, 1889. **O3. C. 12.**

YEITAKU, Sensai.—Bambutsu Hinagata Gwafu. Book of Designs; by Sensai Yeitaku, engraved by Ōtsuka Tetsugorō. *Cuts.* Vols. 1, 4, 5, of a set of 5. (9×6) Tōkyō, 1880–82. **O3. E. 18.**

YOSHINOBU, Ikeda.—Kwakuzen Zuko. Illustrated Account of Decorated Leather-work. Compiled and published by Ikeda Yoshinobu. *Cuts, col.* (14×9), 1845 (2nd year of Kōkwa). **O4. F. 2.**

SHUNKŌ, Odagiri —Narumi-gata. Examples of ornament from ancient. relics, temple treasures, foreign works of art, etc.; by Shunkō Odagiri (at the age of 73). *Cuts.* 5 vols. (9 × 6) Nagoya, 1883. O5. C. 25.

SUWARA. Shūgiōku bukan. Guide to the noble & military families of Japan (giving badge ceremonial spear,residence,income & numbe of retainers.) Pub. by Suwara. cuts. $(2\frac{3}{4}\times$ Tōkyō,Genji 1 (A.D.1864). 08.C.11.

TOMOKI, Taguchi.—Yatsuo no tsubaki. Designs copied from old costumes, vessels, etc. *Cuts, col.* (13 × 9).
O3. A. 3.

A modern reprint.

TANAKA Kikuo.—I-ro-ha-biki Mon-chō. Alphabetic list of Japanese badges. engr. (3×6½) Tōkyō,Meiji 14 (A.D.1881) 08.C.13.

tion from She Seisei Kokan (Chinese Si-tsing-ku-
kien, the Antiquaries' Mirror from a serene Gallery)
a work on Antiqities in 40 vols.compiled by order
of the Emperor Kien Lung (1736-95). Examples selected
as patterns for Japanese artists. 2 vols. engr.(11x8)
Tokyo,1892.   05.A.19.
ITCHŌ, Hanabusa (a pupil of).- Shiokunin dzukushi.
  Pictures of Japanese artisans. cuts. vol.2 of 2.
  (10½x7¼) Tōkyō (late 18th.C.)   08.A.7

> MINKŌ, Tachibana.—Saigwa Shokunin Burui. Various
> Artisans at work, with brief descriptions. Illustrated by
> Tachibana Minkō. *Cuts, col.* 2 vols. in 1. (11×8)
> Yedo, 1770.   **O5. A. 14.**
>
> Another copy, large paper. Vol. 1 of a set.
>   **O5. A. 13.**

1729. see section 1 p.9.

CHIHAYA,Jōchō. Yamato-no-Hikari. The Glory of Japan.
  illustrations & descriptions of ancient art objects
  in the temple Horiuji. Copied by Sudzuki Kinsen.
  3 vols. engr.tinted.(11x7) Nara,1895.   05.A.20
     with m.s. descr. of objects in Eng.
INABA Shinyemon (Tsurio)-Sōken Kishō. Handbook to
  various famous arts. With a preface by Kondo Tadazo
  Vol.1. General remarks.11.111.1V.V. Genealogies of
  famous metal-workers &tsuba makers.V1.leather &
  Inro makers. V11. Makers of Netsuke, seals &Ojime.
  cuts. 7 vols. (9x6½) Ōsaka,Temmei 1. (A.D.1781)
                                           08.C.2.
KUROKAWA,Mayori. Kohitsu Ryochū, & Kwashiwagi Kwai-
  ichiro.- Kōgei shiriō. History of the Industrial Arts
  of Weaving ,Masonry,Pottery,Woodwork,Leather,Metal-
  work & Lacquer. 2 vols. (7½x5) Tōkyō Museum 1877.
                                           08.C.7.
MASANOBU,KITAO (Iwase Samuru). Kōhōshū. Collection of
  Japanese Antiquities. 4 vols.(all printed) cuts (10x7)
  n.p. n.d. modern reprint of work 1813-15. 03.A.7.
SHINRI.Yamataka.-Shūkindo Kanshō Yokyō. Critical Remin-
  iscence of Shūkindo. cuts,col. vol 1 of a set.(12x9)
  Tōkyō,1881.   05.A.23.
  Shūkindo is the house title of the author.This is th
  coll. of what he deemed to be the best among many ar
  productions brought for his crit.by several famous a
  whose names were concealed on the occasion.

SECTION IV.—HANDICRAFTS AND TRADES.

(GENERAL COLLECTIONS.)

See also Section VII.—COSTUME.

HIROSHIGE, Ryūsai.—Shoshoku Gwatsū. Book of Designs. *Cuts, col.* Vols. 1–3 of a set. (7 × 5). **O4. C. 15.**

HOKUSAI.—Hokusai Mangwa. Collection of Sketches. *Cuts, col.* 14 vols. (2 copies of vol. 5, 1 with extra cuts). (9 × 6), 1834. **O3. E. 8.**

MORIKUNI, Tachibana.—Yehon Tsūhōshi. Pictures of various scenes of Trades, Amusements, Birds, Flowers, etc., with notes. *Cuts.* Vols. 1, 2, 6, of a set of 10. (9 × 6) Naniwa (Ōsaka), 1721. *1729.* **O3. D. 25.**

POEMS.—Yehon Minanogawa. Verses from famous Poems. *Cuts.* Vol. 1, and part of vol. 2 (bound together), of a set of 3. (9 × 6). **O5. D. 21.**

TESSAI, Hirase.—Nihon Sankai Meibutsu Zuye. Description of the chief Products of Japan. Illustrated by Shōsuiken Hasegawa Mitsunobu. Compiled by Hirase Tessai. *Cuts.* 5 vols. (10 × 7) Ōsaka, 1797. **O3. C. 13.**

TRADES.—Shokunin Uta-awase. Poems on the various Trades and Crafts, with illustrations *Cuts.* 3 vols. (11 × 7). **O5. B. 11.**

——— Yedo Shokunin Uta-awase. Notes on various Trades in Yedo. *Cuts.* (10 × 7), 1808. **O5. B. 12.**

-KWA.- Koku-Kwa (National Flower). A selection the best examples of Japanese Fine Art,with lanatory Notes by various authors,repros.of ous Pictures & illustrations of typical specimens Industrial Art. Ed. by Rokusaburo Yamamoto & other tes,some col . & ill. in the text.(16x11) Tōkyō.18 an ed. with some English text. **O2.E.1**

SECTION IV*a.*—TEXTILE FABRICS AND EMBROIDERY.

See also Section VII.—Costume.

Inscriptions.—Shūko Jisshu. Heiki (Weapons). Inscriptions on Banners. *Cuts.* 5 vols. (15 × 10).

O4. A. 6.

Nakajima, Tanjirō.—Hinagata Yado-no-ume. Patterns of Ladies' Dresses. *Cuts.* Vol. 3. (10 × 7) Naniwa (Ōsaka), 1730.

O5. B. 13.

Silkworm Cultivation.—Yōsan Hiroku. Secrets of Silkworm Breeders. *Cuts.* Vol. 2 of a set of 3. (10 × 7).

O3. C. 14.

Albums of Prints in Colour.

Album.—Portraits of Women, Theatrical Characters, Illustrations of the Silkworm Industry, etc.; by Keisai (Yeisen), Kunichika, Kunimasa (Ichijusai, Baidō), Kunisada (Toyokuni 2nd, Kachōrō), Kunisada 2nd (Baichōrō), Kuniyoshi (Ichiyūsai), Ōsai, Toyokuni, Yoshichika (Chōkarō, Ikkeisai), and Yoshifuji (Ippōsai). *40 sheets.* (14 × 9¾).

O2. A. 21.

———— Theatrical Characters. Portraits of Women, Illustrations of the Silkworm Industry, Twelve scenes from the drama "Chūshingura," etc., by Fusatane (Isshōsai), Hiroshige, Hokuyei (Shunkōsai), Ichimaru (Jippōsha), Keisai (Yeisen, Ippitsuan), Kiyomitsu, Kunihiro, Kunisada (Toyokuni 2nd, Ichiyōsai, Kokuteisha, Kachōrō), Kuniyasu (Ippōsai), Kuniyoshi (Chōōrō, Ichiyūsai), Nobukatsu, Sadafusa (Gokitei), Sadahiro (Gorakutei), Sadayoshi (Kwaishuntei), Shigeharu (Gyokuryūtei), Shunshō, Toyokuni, Yeishō (Shinsai), Yoshifuji (Ippōsai), and Yoshitora (Ichimōsai). *60 sheets.* (14½ × 10).

O1. C. 33.

Albums of Specimens of Fabrics.

Album, Textiles; 199 specimens. (16 × 16)

O1. F. 1.

KURIBARA,Magonojo.- Senko-fu-ryaku. Biographical
   list of Japanese workers in metal. Facs.sigs.
   $(3\frac{1}{4}\times7\frac{1}{2})$ Tōkyō, 1844.   08.C.10.

Note. All the volume entitled 'Shuko Jisshu' are
   by the painter Bunchō.

MATSUOKA Shiben.—Shōzoku Shokubun Zuye. Patterns
   of textiles used in the the State costumes of the Emperor,
   Imperial family, and Court nobles. Compiled by Matsuoka Shiben.   New ed.   *Cuts, some col.* (11×8),
   1815.   **O5. A. 16.**

   This work was first compiled for private circulation only, in (?)
   1801, which date the preface bears. The present edition consisted of
   200 copies.

GANARI, Kodama.- Shinsen Kodai Moyōkagami. A new
   coll. of typical designs (of Textile fabrics) of
   ancient times. cuts,col. vol.2 of a set. (10x7)
   Tōkyō, 1884.   05.A.28.
      with detailed M.S. descr,in English.
JNSHO,Katsukawa & SHIGEMASA, Kitao.- Kaiko
   yashinaigusa. The cultivation of silk-worms. cut
   col. Tokyo,Temmei 6, 1st.month (A.D.1786)
                                  08.A.3.
KIZAWA, Kiyoshi,- Kodai moyōshū. coll. of old
   patterns from textiles. cuts. 2 vols. $(5\times7\frac{1}{2})$
   Tōkyō,1881.   08.C.8.

LBUM,Textiles; 32 specimens of old brocades &
   woven Silks. (4x6)   04.D.18.
LBUM,Textiles; 74 specimens of Brocade,Woven
      Silks & Embroidery. (6x5)   04.D.19.
LBUM,Textiles; 22 specimens of old brocades and
      woven Silks. (10x8)   05.A.32.
LBUM,Textiles; 41 specimens of old brocades.
   (10x8)   05.A.33.
LBUM,Textiles; 36 specimens of old brocades.
   (8x10)   05.A.34.
LBUM,Textiles; 73 specimens of old brocades.
   (9x8)   05.A.35.
LBUM,Textiles; 40 specimens of old brocade,
   some stencilled & embroidered. 2 vols.
   $(9\frac{3}{4}\times7\frac{1}{2})$ 05.A.36,37.
LBUM,Textiles; 77 specimens of brocades.

ALBUM, Textiles; Nioki-no-nishiki.—Samples of silk. 100
  specimens of Silk Velvets, Plushes, etc. Vol. 2 of a private
  collection. (14 × 9) Early xixth cent. O2. E. 6.

YAMANAKA Kichirobei.- Moyo hinagata **Miyako-no-Nishiki,**
  Brocade of the Capital (Kyoto). Designs for embroidered,stencilled or painted robes. cuts,col.
  3 vols. (10x7) Osaka, 1890. a reprint. 05.F.15.
YAMANAKA Kichirobei.- Moyo Hinagata Naniwa-no-ume.
  Plum blossom of Naniwa. Designs for embroidered,
  stencilled or painted robes. cuts,col. 3 vols.
  (10x7) Osaka,1886.   03.A.5.
    Designs fashionable in the city of Naniwa (Osaka),
  which is always associated with plum-blossom.

POTTERY.—Shogwa. Utsuwa-ye Tehon. Designs for
  Pottery and Porcelain; painting and caligraphy. *Cuts,*
  col. (7 × 5) Yedo, 1834.   O4. D. 10.

Katsushika Taito/

ALBUM, Textiles; 108 specimens of Woven Silks and Brocades. (12 × 15). **O2. E. 3.**

—— Textiles; 23 specimens of Woven and Embroidered Silks. (14 × 9). **O2. E. 4.**

—— Textiles; 568 specimens. (14 × 10). **O2. E. 5.**

—— Textiles; 323 small specimens of Woven Silks. (6 × 5). **O4. C. 26.**

—— Textiles; 168 specimens of Silks, Embroideries and Brocades. (10 × 8). **O5. C. 23.**

SECTION IVb.—POTTERY AND PORCELAIN.

CHIBA, Ryūboku.—Hyakki Zukai. Drawings of Flower Vases, with full descriptions and owners' names. Vols. 1, 3, of a set of 3. *Cuts.* (9 × 6), 1773. **O3. D. 26.**

INSCRIPTIONS.—Shūko Jisshu. Inscriptions on Monuments, Tiles, etc. *Cuts.* 13 vols. (15 × 10). **O4. A. 5.**

SHŌKO RŌJIN, *pseud.*—Kohon Meibutsu Ruishū. Collection and Records of famous utensils for the most part used in the Tea Ceremony. Compiled by Shōko Rōjin. *Cuts, some col.* 4 vols., in 18 parts. (9 × 6), 1787.
O3. D. 27.

SECTION IVc.—METAL WORK.

Note.—For ARMS AND ARMOUR *see* Section VIIa.— MILITARY COSTUME.

HOKUSAI, Gwakyō Rōjin.—Yehon Shin Hinagata. Original Designs, Plans and Working Drawings, for Engineers and others, by Hokusai (in his 77th year). *Cuts.* Vol. 1 of a set of 3. (9 × 6), 1836. **O3. D. 22.**

HOKUSAI, Katsushika Isai.—Kwachō Sansui Saigwa Zushiki. Designs for Art Metal-work. *Cuts.* Vols. 3, 4, of a set of 5. (5 × 7) Yedo, 1863–64. **O4. D. 2.**

INSCRIPTIONS.—Shūko Jisshu. Copies of Inscriptions on Bells, Lamp-posts, Vessels, etc. *Cuts.* 9 vols. (15 × 10).
O4. A. 4.

METAL WORK.—Shūko Jisshu. Metal work. Mirrors, with cases, Bells, etc. *Cuts.* 3 vols. (15 × 10). **O4. A. 7.**

SECTION IV*d.*—MISCELLANEOUS CRAFTS AND TRADES (NOT INCLUDED IN *a*, *b*, or *c*).

Note.—The ALBUMS classified in Sections VII, and VII*b*, contain a number of incidental illustrations of FURNITURE and MUSICAL INSTRUMENTS.

BIRDS.—Studies of Bird-form. *Cuts, tinted.* (5 × 8).
O4. D. 1.

HORSE FURNITURE.—Shūko Jisshu. Heiki (Weapons). Harness, etc. *Cuts.* 3 vols. (15 × 10). **O4. A. 8.**

KURIHARA [Nobumitsu.]—Patterns of Bridles. *Cuts. col.* (11 × 7) 1834. **O5. B. 9.**

LADIES.—Book of useful Information for Ladies, with illustrations of Domestic Scenes, Poets and Poetesses, household Furniture, etc. *Cuts.* 9 vols. (11 × 7 *p. c. 1750*)
O5. B. 16.

MUSICAL INSTRUMENTS.—Shūko Jisshu. Operatic and Musical Instruments, Masks, etc. *Cuts.* Vols. 2–6 of a set of 6. (15 × 10). **O4. A. 9.**

NORIKUNI Ochiai.—Book of Designs for Carpenters; by Norikuni Ochiai, engraved by Sentarō Yegawa. 2 ed. *Cuts.* Parts 2 of vol. 1; and 1, 2, of vol. 2. (5 × 7), 1876, (9th year of Meiji). **O4. D. 6.**

TEA.—Tea cultivation and Domestic Scenes. 10 ff. *Col. prints on linen.* (7 × 10). **O4. E. 7.**

WRITING MATERIALS.—Shūko Jisshu. Illustrations of Writing Materials, etc. *Cuts.* 2 vols. (15 × 10).
O4. A. 10.

YOSHINOBU, Ikeda.—Kwakuzen Zuko. Illustrated Account of Decorated Leather-work. Compiled and published by Ikeda Yoshinobu. *Cuts, col.* (14 × 9), 1845 (2nd year of Kōkwa). **O4. F. 2.**

NARIAKI, Noda.—Kinkò Kantei Hiketsu. Secrets in examining metal work. Guide to the detection of forgeries, in metal work of the Gotō school. Illustrated by the author and Takase Tomohiro, engraved by Yegawa Tomekichi. *Cuts.* 2 vols. (11×7) Yedo. 1819. **O5. A. 12.**

It appears to have been intended to deal with the Yokoya and Nara schools in a later work.

KONDŌ Morishige.- Kingin dzuroku. Ancient gold & silver coins. cuts,col. 7 vols.(8½x5¾) (?) Yedo. Bunkwa 7.(A.D. 1810)   08.C.6.

CHIHARU,Takashima,-Kodzu ruiji chō-donobu..ill.of ancient writing materials,implements etc. cut. vol.1 of 31 or 32. (10x7½) Tokyo,Bunsei 6. (A.D. 1823)   08.8.12.
    Chiharu died Ansei 6. (A.D.1859) aged 83.

LACQUER.- Kodai makiye hinagata. Models of old lacquer work. cuts,col. Vols.1,2 of a series. (10¾x7¾) n,p. n.d.   08.8.3
    Probably published at Tōkyō at the end 18th.C.

LEATHER.—78 specimens of stamped and lacquered leather. (*Average*, 5¼×7¼).   **J 4814.**

With collection of Japanese Prints.

———— 42 specimens of printed or stencilled leather, formerly used for the lining of armour. (*In book*, 17×10¾).   **J 4815.**

With collection of Japanese Prints.

IKUNI, Ochiai Taigo.- Simpen Ramma Hinagata. A new compilation of patterns for Open-work; all of the Enshū School. cuts. 2 vols. (5x7) Tōkyō 1852.   04.D.15.

YOSHIMASA, Ōoka.—Makiye Daizen. Designs for lacquer-work, with a brief account of the art. Written and illustrated by Ōoka Yoshimasa, called Shunsen. *Cuts.* Vols. 1, 3, 5 of a set of 5. (11×7) Naniwa (Ōsaka), 1759.   **O3. F. 16.**

OKA,Hayato.- Ranma dzushiki. Patterns of wood-carving; for the panels over the screens of a house. cuts. 3 vols. (7½x10) Tōkyō,Kiohō 19,1st. month.(A.D. 1734)   08.8.9.

KUBOTA **Beisen** & SOGAKU, Nagai. Dzuan Fukusa
    Awase. Designs for Fukusa by various artists.
    cuts,col. 2 vols. (10x6) Tōkyō 1894. 05.A.27.
    (Fukusa are silken cloths used for covering small
    objects of value,ceremonial presents,etc.)
SHUNSEN, Hokkyō.- Makiye taizen. Pictures of the
    different kinds of lacquer. illustrated by
    Hokkyō Shunsen. cuts. 5 vols. (9¾x7) Tōkyō,
    Horeki 9 (A.D. 1759)   08.B.8.
        a modern reprint.

Bakin. Takezawa. See Regomey. Trans. into French of
        a novel by him.

SECTION V.—ILLUSTRATED BOOKS.

(POEMS, STORIES, BOOKS OF ETIQUETTE, MORALS, ETC.)

AESOP.—Tsūzoku Aesop Monogatari. The Fables of Aesop. Translated into Japanese by A. Watanabe. *Cuts, tinted.* 6 vols. (9 × 6), 1873. **O5. D. 1.**

AKATSUKI, Keimeisha, Kanenari.—Ibuki Monogatari. A Novel; illustrated by Keimeisha Akatsuki Kanenari. *Cuts.* 5 vols. (9 × 6). **O5. D. 2.**

BAKIN.—Kimpeibai. A Novel; illustrated by Kunisada. Vol. 5, part 2; vol. 8, in 2 parts; vol. 9. part 1. *Cuts.* (7 × 5), 1841–42. **O4. E. 1.**

ENCYCLOPÆDIA.—Joyō Bunshō Yukikai Buri. Book of useful Information; Letter writing, moral Verses, celebrated Poems, etc. *Cuts.* (11 × 7) Yedo, 1833.
O5. B. 14.

HANZAN, Matsugawa.—Hisago-no-tsuru. Collection of humorous Verses, with Parodies on original Poems; illustrated by Matsugawa Hanzan. *Cuts, col.* (9 × 6), 1851. **O3. E. 19.**

HARUNOBU, Suzuki.—Poems, illustrated by Suzuki Harunobu. *Cuts.* The last of a set of 2 or 3 vols. (8 × 6) 1763 (13th year of Hōryaku). **O5. D. 3.**

HENYEI.—Gentai Gwafu. Text book of Views, Trees, Figures, Buildings, etc., from the Chinese. *Cuts.* 5 vols. (10 × 7) Yedo, 1806. **O5. B. 15.**

HISTORY.—Yehon Zen Taiheiki. Short history of the rebellion in the year of Tenkei, of Taira-no Masakado and Fujiwara Sumitomo. *Cuts.* 5 vols. (9 × 6).
O5. D. 4.

HOKUSAI.—Yehon Suikoden. The Hundred and Eight Heroes and Heroines from the Chinese novel "Suikoden." *Cuts.* (9 × 6), 1829. **O3. E. 21.**

———— Yehon Sakigake. Pictures of noted Japanese and Chinese Personages; by Hokusai (at the age of 76), engraved by Sugita Kinsuke and Yegawa Tomekichi. *Cuts.* Vol. 1 of a set of 4. (9 × 6), 1835. **O3. E. 20.**

HOKUSAI.—Yehon Wakan-no Homare. Noted Japanese and Chinese Heroes; by Hokusai (at the age of 76). *Cuts, tinted.* (9 × 6), 1850. **O3. E. 22.**

Another copy. *Cuts.* (9 × 6), 1850. **O3. E. 23.**

IZAWA Matajirō.—Gwasan Tokonoyama. Poems; engraved by Izawa Matajirō. *Cuts, col.* Vol. 2 of a set of 3. (9 × 6). **O5. D. 5.**

KEISAI Yeisen.—Yeiyū Gwashi. Portraits of Heroes and Heroines. *Cuts.* (9 × 6), 1836. **O5. D. 6.**

KIMIYOSHI, Ikuyo.—Nana Komachi Monogatari. A Novel, written and illustrated by Ikuyo Kimiyoshi. *Cuts, col.* Vol. 1. of a set of (?) 7. (9 × 6). **O5. D. 7.**

KINSUI, Shōtei.—Takagi-no Jitsuden. A Novel: Life of Takagi Oriyemon. *Cuts.* 2 vols., each in 5 parts. (9 × 6), 1852. **O5. D. 8.**

KIRAKU, Nanritei.—Nijushi-kō Zuye. The Twenty-four Models of Filial Piety (from the Chinese); compiled by Nanritei Kiraku, illustrated by Katsushika Taito. *Cuts.* (9 × 6), 1822. **O5. D. 9.**

KIYOTSUNE.—The Twenty-four Models of Filial Piety (from the Chinese). Illustrated by Kiyotsune. *Cuts, col.* 2 vols. (8 × 6). **O5. D. 10.**

KŌSUISAI, Kitao.—Yehon Yaso Ujikawa. Famous Japanese and Chinese Heroes, with verses of humorous poetry; illustrated by Kitao Kōsuisai. *Cuts.* 3 vols., bound in 1. (9 × 6), 1786. **O5. D. 11.**

KUNIYOSHI.—Illustrations to the Hundred Poems. *Cuts, col.* (14 × 9½). **O4. F. 3.**

LADIES.—Book of useful Information for Ladies, with illustrations of Domestic Scenes, Poets and Poetesses, household Furniture, etc. *Cuts.* 2½ vols. (11 × 7). **O5. B. 16.**

MATORA, Ōishi.—Onna Shōgaku. Book of Useful Information for Girls. Illustrated by Ōishi Matora. Engraved by Higuchi Yohei. 3 ed. *Cuts.* (10 × 7) Ōsaka, 1852. **O3. C. 15.**

MITSUNOBU, Hasegawa.—Misao. Moral Lessons for Girls; illustrated by Hasegawa Mitsunobu. *Cuts, col.* (9 × 6). **O3. E. 24.**

KI.- The Kojiki. Records of Ancient Matters. A
.story of Japan written in the 18th.C. 3 vols.
$10\frac{1}{4}\times7\frac{1}{4}$) Kyoto,Kwanyei,21 (A.D.1643)   O3.A.8.
This is the earliest history of Japan. It has
en trans. by B.H. Chamberlain. (Suppl. vol.to
l.X. of the Trans. of the Asiatic Society of Japan

X

KWANJAKU.—Kwanjaku Tsuizen. A volume of poems and
essays, illustrated by various artists ; published in
memory of Kwanjaku, a celebrated actor, by the
Kintsusha, a literary society. *Cuts, col.* (9 × 6) 1852
(Kayei 5th, 2nd month).   **O3. F. 20.**

NIHONGI.-Nihon Shoki (or Nihongi). Chronicles
of Japan,compiled in the 8th.C. 24 (in 3) vols
(10x7) Kyōto (?) 1599.   03.A.6.
 A translation by W.G. Aston,was published by
Japan Society,2 vols,1896.

MORAL LESSONS.—Yehon Jitsugokyō. Moral lessons ; with notes. *Cuts.* 3 vols. (9 × 6) Naniwa (Ōsaka), 1802.
O3. E. 25.

MORAL STORY.—Hana-no Tsuyu. A Moral Story. *Cuts.* 1 vol. (9 × 6). **O3. E. 26.**

MORIKAWA, Yasuyuki.—Yamato Monogatari. A Novel; illustrated by the author. *Cuts.* 5 vols. (9 × 6).
O5. D. 12.

MORIKUNI, Tachibana.—Gwayen. Illustrations of Japanese and Chinese Poems. *Cuts.* 6 vols. (10 × 7).
O5. B. 17.

———— Yehon Kojidan. Illustrated Stories of celebrated Views, and distinguished Personages, in Japan and China. *Cuts.* 8 vols., (vol. 5 in 2 parts). (9 × 6) Ōsaka, 1714.
O5. E. 1.

OMOTE-NO KUROTO, *pseud.*—Yamato Kantan. Humorous Story. *Cuts, col.* Vol. 1 of a set. (9 × 6). **O5. D.13.**

ONO-NO KOMACHI.—Yehon Sonarematsu. Poems by Ono-no Komachi. Illustrated by Nishikawa Sukenobu. *Cuts.* 3 vols. in 2. (9 × 6), 1736. **O5. D. 14.**

PHRASES.—Witty Phrases. *Cuts.* (9 × 6). **O5. D. 45.**

POEMS. — Fūshishū. Verses of humorous Poetry on various subjects of the time, with illustrations. *Cuts.* 2 vols. (11 × 7), 1729. **O5. B. 18.**

———— Poems. *Cuts.* (9 × 6). **O5. D. 23.**

———— Poems. *Cuts.* (9 × 6). **O5. D. 24.**

———— Poems and short Stories (fragments from various books bound together). *Cuts.* (9 × 6). **O5. D. 25.**

———— Sugataye. One hundred verses of Poetry. *Cuts.* Vol. 3. (9 × 6). **O5. D. 15.**

———— Tōshisen Yehon. Explanation of Chinese Poems. *Cuts.* Vol. 3. (9 × 6). **O5. D. 16.**

———— Yehon Biwako. Verses from the Genji Monogatari *Cuts.* Vol. 2 of a set of 3. (9 × 6). **O5. D. 17.**

POEMS.—Yehon Chitose-yama. Poems and Moral Lessons. Pages 9–13 of vol. 2, bound with vol. 3, of a set of 3. *Cuts.* (9 × 6). **O5. D. 18.**

———— Yehon Chiyo-no-matsu. Poems. *Cuts.* Vol. 2 of a set of 3. (9 × 6). **O5. D. 19.**

———— Yehon Fuji-no-hakama. Verses and short Stories, from the "Genji Monogatari." *Cuts.* Vol. 2 of a set of 3. (9 × 6). **O5. D. 20.**

———— Yehon Mina-no-gawa. Verses from famous poems. *Cuts.* Vol. 1, and part of vol. 2, bound together, of a set of 3. (9 × 6). **O5. D. 21.**

———— Yūkyō Shōzōshū, vol. 2; Imayō Gwazōshū, vol. 3; Meisho Yūran, vol. 3, part 2. Poems, with illustrations. (Portions of 3 works bound together.) *Cuts.* (9 × 6). **O5. D. 22.**

RASAN.—Yehon Senga-no-ura. Explanation of Proverbial Phrases, illustrated by Terai. *Cuts.* Vol. 1 of a set of 3. (9 × 6). **O5. D. 26.**

SENKWA, Ryūtei. — Ashikaga-ginu Tezome-no Murasaki. Book of Stories. Each frontispiece, and vols. 6–9, illustrated by Toyokuni (Ichiyōsai), the remainder by Kunisada 2nd. *Cuts, some col.* Vols. 6–16, 18, bound in 6. (7 × 5) Yedo, 1850–56. **O4. E. 2.**

SESSUIKEN.—Haikai Shokugyō Zukushi. Poems on various Subjects. Collected by Sessuiken. *Cuts, tinted.* 2 vols. (9 × 6), 1842. **O5. E. 2.**

SHINZŌ.—Heigo waka, Yehon Kame-no-o-yama. Poems by different Nobles, Ladies, Warriors, etc., with supplementary short stories, quoted from the "Heike Monogatari." Illustrated by Nishikawa Sukenobu, Jitokusō, and engraved by Niwa Shōbei. *Cuts.* 2 vols. (9 × 6), 1747 (4th year of Yenkyō). **O5. D. 28.**

SHUMBOKU.—Boku-ō Shingwa. Anecdotes of noted Personages in China and Japan. Illustrated by Shumboku. *Cuts.* Vols. 1, 4, 5, of a set. (11 × 7). **O5. B. 19.**

SHUNSUI, Tamenaga.—Usuomokage Maboroshi Nikki. Book of Stories. Illustrated by Kunisada 2nd. *Cuts.* (7 × 5), 1858. **O4. E. 3.**

SHUNSHŌ, Katsugawa.—Nishiki Hiakunin Isshu. The
Hundred Poets with their poems. Engraved by Inouye
Shinshichirō. *Cuts, col.* (11 × 8) 1775 (Anyei 4th).

O5. F. 7.

There are six supplementary illustrations referring to the Rokkasen
(the six poets genii) with their poems. The work is signed Ririn
Katsugawa Yūsuke Fuji (of Fujiwara) Shunshō. Ririn is the name
of a studio.

SUKENOBU, Nishikawa.—Yehon Yamato Hiji. Book of famous Views, noted Personages, etc., with short stories; illustrated by Nishikawa Sukenobu. *Cuts.* 9 vols. and supplement (9 × 6) Kyōto, 1716-42. **O5. E. 33.**

SHŪSUI, Shimokōbe.—Iroha-uta Yeshō. Verses of Poetry on moral subjects, for Children; illustrated by Shimokōbe Shūsui. *Cuts.* 3 vols, in 1. (9 × 6), 1775. **O5. E. 4.**

———— Yehon Amayadori. Moral Story; illustrated by Shimokōbe Shūsui. *Cuts.* 3 vols. (9 × 6), 1780.
O5. E. 3.

SONGS.—Kouta Kanoko. A Reprint of Popular Songs, of about the period of 1660 (3rd year of Manji). *Cuts.* (9 × 6), 1819 (2nd year of Bunsei). **O5. E. 5.**

STORIES.—Deirichō. Illustrated Story Book for Children. *Cuts.* (9 × 6). **O5. E. 7.**

———— Gei-bi Kōgi Den. Stories of Personages famous for their Filial Piety, in the provinces of Aki and Bingo. *Cuts.* 9 vols. (9 × 6) Hiroshima, 1797. **O5. E. 6.**

———— Gempei. Short stories of Warriors. Rinrin. Verses of comic poetry, with short stories. (Portions of 2 books bound together.) *Cuts.* (9 × 6). **O5. E. 8.**

SUGITA Kinsuke.—Tōshisen Yehon. Illustrations of Chinese Poetry. Engraved by Sugita Kinsuke. *Cuts.* 5 vols. (9 × 6), 1791. **O5. E. 19.**

SUKENOBU, Nishikawa, Bunkwadō.—Yehon Kagami Hyakushu. Moral Poems; illustrated by N Sukenobu. *Cuts.* Vol. 3 of a set of 3. (9 × 6), 1739. **O5. E. 13. /2.**

———— Zoku Hyakushu. Verses of moral Poetry; illustrated by N. Sukenobu. *Cuts.* Vol. 3 of a set of 3. (9 × 6), 1739. **O5. E. 9.**

———— Yehon Chitoseyama. Verses of Poetry, with short Stories. Illustrated by N. Sukenobu. *Cuts.* 3 vols. (9 × 6), 1740. **O5. E. 10.**

———— Yehon Tsurezuregusa. Book of Stories; illustrated by N. Sukenobu. *Cuts.* 3 vols. bound in 1. (10 × 7) Miyako (Kyōto), 1740. **O5. B. 21.**

———— Yehon Muro-no-ume (2 parts). Yehon Tokitsukaze (2 parts). Humorous Stories. Illustrated by N. Sukenobu. *Cuts.* 4 vols. bound together (9 × 6), 1788. **O5. E. 14.**

SUKENOBU, Nishikawa, Bunkwadō.—Yehon Ike-no-kokoro. Moral Poems, illustrated by N. Sukenobu. *Cuts.* Vol. 1 of a set of 3. (9 × 6), 17 ..   **O5. E. 11.**

—— Yehon Mina-no-gawa. Verses of Poetry; illustrated by N. Sukenobu. *Cuts.* Vol. 1 of a set of 3. (9 × 6), 17 ..   **O5. E. 13.**

—— Yehon Narabi-no-oka. Book of various Scenes from old stories. *Cuts.* (10 × 7).   **O5. B. 20.**

—— Yehon Tamakazura. Poems, illustrated by N. Sukenobu. Vol. 1 of a set of 3. *Cuts.* (9 × 6).
     O5. E. 15.

—— Yehon Tsukuba-yama. Verses of Poetry by different famous poets, on various subjects; illustrated by N. Sukenobu. *Cuts.* Vol. 3 of a set of 3. (9 × 6).
     O5. E. 16.

SUKETADA, Nishikawa.—Hyōkin Mojirigusa. Humorous verses of Poetry. *Cuts.* 1 vol. (9 × 6).   **O5. E. 17.**

SUKEYO, Kwagetsutei Yūkwōken.—Yehon. Story book. 1 vol.

Yega ogusa. Story book. 1 vol.

Chiye-no-umi. Puzzle picture. 1 vol.

Story book. 2 vols.
     4 works in 1, illustrated by Kwagetsutei Sukeyo. *Cuts.* (9 × 6), 1761.   **O5. E. 18.**

—— Niwaka Zukushi, Odoke Sairei, Shin-karukuchi hatsu-akinai. Yehon Miyo-no-haru. Humorous stories, illustrated by Yūkwōken Sukeyo. *Cuts.* 5 vols. in 1. (9 × 6), 1763.   **O5. E. 20.**

TANEHIKO, Ryūtei,—Yakko-no Koman. A Novel; illustrated by Yūyūsai Tōsen. *Cuts.* 2 vols., with 2 supplementary vols. (9 × 5), 1807.   **O4. E. 5.**

—— Inu-no Sōshi. A Novel in easy words for children; from the original "Hakkenden," by Bakin. Illustrated by Toyokuni (vols. 1–5, 7–22), Sadahide (6), Kunisada (24–28, 30–41), Kunitsuna (42–48), Kuniteru (49, 50), Kunimasa (51, 54), Kunitoshi (52), Kunitaki (53). *Cuts, some col.* 52 vols. of a set. (7 × 5), 1849.   **O4. E. 4.**

Good copy.

Portion of vol. 1 only. last page wanting.

TACHIBANA,Mochiyo.- Hokuetsu Kidan. Curious
    Tales from the northern province of Yechigo.
    Ill. by Hokusai. vols.1-4,6 of a set of 6.
    cuts.($8\frac{3}{4}$x6) n.p. Bunkwa 8 (A.D. 1811)
                                O3.A.10.

TAKAI, Ranzan.—Tôshisen Yehon. Illustrated notes on
    the Chinese collection of poems, Tôshisen. Illustrated
    by Suikei; engraved by Sugita Kinsuke. *Cuts.* 5 vols.
    (9 × 6) Yedo, 1832.   **O5. C. 26.**

TEIKA.—Kin-yō-shō. The hundred poems selected by Teika; supplemented with precepts for women, matrimonial customs, etc. Illustrated by Ishida Giokuden. *Cuts, col.* (10 × 7) Ōsaka. **O3. F. 19.**

A reprint from blocks first published in 1835.

YEITAKU,Kobayashi Senshai.- A collection of 'Childrens' Sports'. 3 pp. 12 col.prints. (9x13) Tōkyō 1888. O4.F.15.

YOSHIHARU, Ogasawara.—Minkan Shihō, Daizen Meiji Shin-Hiakunin Isshu. Indispensable treasures, enlarged and complete, with the hundred poems newly selected in Meiji period. *Cuts.* (9 × 6) Tōkyō, 1880. **O5. C. 27.**

TANEHIKO, Ryūtei.—Katsushika Monogatari. Book of
Stories; illustrated by Kunisada. *Cuts.* (7 × 5), 1865.
O4. E. 3.

TANEKIYO.—Suiko Gwaden. Short lives of the Hundred
and Eight Heroes from the Chinese novel "Suikoden",
composed by Tanekiyo, illustrated by Hokkei. *Cuts,*
col. 3 vols. (9 × 6), 1856. **O5. E. 21.**

TEIKAKYŌ.—Shūko Jisshu. Poems. (15 × 10). **O4. B. 1.**

TERAZAWA Masatsugu.—Tales for Children. Illustrated
by Terazawa Masatsugu. *Cuts.* (9 × 6). **O5. E. 22.**

TOGETSU, Hokumei. — Tsurugaoka Yahazu Daimon.
Sketches of the Life of Kajiwara Kagetoki. *Cuts.*
6 vols. (9 × 6). **O5. D. 29.**

TOKIYORI Saimyōji. — Shimizu-no Ike. Moral Poems.
Illustrated by Nishikawa Sukenobu. *Cuts.* 3 vols.
(9 × 6), 1734. **O5. E. 23.**

TOKUSHŌ, Goryūtei.—Santo Yakusha Suikoden. Romance
of the Hundred and Eight Heroes and Heroines at
Kyōto, Ōsaka, and Yedo, after the Chinese novel
"Suikoden." Composed by Goryūtei Tokushō, illustrated by Gototei Kunisada. *2 cuts, col.* Vol. 1 of a
series. (9 × 6) Yedo, 1829. **O5. E. 24.**

WAKABAYASHI, Kuzumichi.—Seishō Shindenki. Life of
the Hero, Katō Kiyomasa, one of the vassals of Toyo-
tomi Hideyoshi. Illustrated by Gyokusanshi, and his
pupil Gyokuhō. *Cuts.* 1st part, containing 5 vols.,
the 5th bound in 2. (10 × 7), 1812. **O3. C. 16.**

SECTION V*a*.—CARICATURES AND HUMOROUS PICTURES.

CARICATURES.—Tobaye Akubi-dome. Humorous Sketches.
Cuts. Vol. 3. (10 × 7) Ōsaka, 1793. **O5. B. 22.**

———— Tobaye Sangokushi. Humorous Drawings of
Amusements, etc. *Cuts.* Vol. 3 of a set of 3. (10 × 7).
O3. C. 17.

KEISAI.—Chōjū Ryaku-gwashiki. Grotesque drawings of Animals, etc., by Keisai, engraved by Shumpūdō Nojiro Ryūko. *Cuts, col.* (10 × 7) Yedo, 1797. **O5. B. 23.**

———— Jimbutsu Ryaku-gwashiki. Grotesque Sketches; by Keisai, engraved by Shumpūdō Nojiro Ryūko. *Cuts, col.* Vol. 3. (10 × 7), 1799. **O5. B. 24.**

KUNIYOSHI, Ichiyūsai.—Kyōgwa Zushiki. Pictures of the Hundred and Eight Heroes and Heroines from the Chinese novel "Suikoden," humorously drawn by Ichiyūsai Kuniyoshi. *Cuts. col.* Vol. 1. (10 × 6) Tōkyō, 1885. **O3. C. 18.**

MATORA, Ōishi.—Sogwa Hyakubutsu. One hundred rough Sketches from Life. *Cuts, col.* Vols. 1, 3, of a set of 3. (9 × 6) Naniwa, 1832. **O5. E. 25.**

POEMS.—Comic verses of Poetry on "Sake." *Cuts, col.* (9 × 6). **O5. E. 26.**

SAMBA, Shikitei.—Ippai Kigen. Comical stories of a Drunkard; by Shikitei Samba, illustrated by Utagawa Toyokuni. *Cuts.* 2 vols. (7 × 5), 1882.3. **O4. E. 6.**
Meiji 11.

YOSHIKAZU, Ichijusai.—Pictures of Warriors by Ichijusai Yoshikazu; and Comical Pictures of the great earthquake in 1855, by unknown artists. *Cuts, col.* (10 × 7). **O5. C. 18.**

In Japan, it was supposed by some people, that the earthquake was caused by cat fish.

YOSHITSUYA. — Scenes from "Hizakurige"; a humorous novel. *Cuts, col.* (7 × 9½). **O3. C. 7.**

ALBUMS OF PRINTS IN COLOUR.

ALBUM. — Humorous pictures and various Scenes with Wrestlers, Acrobats, Warriors, etc.; by Hirokage, Hiroshige, Joshū, Kunisada 2nd (Baichōrō), Kuniyoshi, Kyōsai, Sadahide (Gountei), Toyokuni, Yoshichika (Ikkeisai), Yoshiharu (Ichibaisai), Yoshimasa (Ippōsai), Yoshimori (Ikkwōsai), and Yoshitora. *71 sheets.* (14 × 9¾). **O1. A. 13.**

IOSAI, Kawanabe.- Kiosai Rakugwa. Humorous
Drawings by Kiosai. cuts,col. vol.2 of a
set of 2. (9x6) Tokyo,1881.   05.A.31.
WAZAN, Watanabe. Isso Hyakutai (Hundred Features
in one sweep; the stroke of the brush being
compared to the sweep of the broom.) Rapid
sketches of men & women. cuts,some tinted.
2 ed. (10x7) Tokyo & Nagoya,1884. 05.A.25.
    1st.ed 1878,but long after the authors death.
TAMARO,Kitagawa.- Waka Yebisu. Scenes of New Years
Day celebrations with humorous poems for the
occasion.(Kyoko). cuts,col. (10x8) Yedo,n.d.
                                08.A.4.

    In the new year everyone is supposed to become
young again. The title is a punning epithet
(Waka=young& poetic) applied to Yebisu,one of
    the Gods of Good Fortune.

TAMARO,Kitagawa.- Kyogetsubo (Full crazy moon)
    Ill. to humorous poems relating to the moon.
    5 col. cuts. 5 sheets of text. (10x7½) Yedo,178
                                08.A.6.

    Kyogetsubo was a famous satirical poet of the
    13th.C. Publisher Koundo.

Broken Up.

Broken Up.

Broken Up.

Broken Up.

Broken Up

ALBUM.—Scenes from the Life of Prince Genji, Views of noted places in Yedo, some with comic accidents, Scenes showing the influence of Good and Evil Spirits upon two youths, etc.; by Hiroshige, Kazukage (Shōsai), Kiku-o, Kunichika, Kunimasa, Toyokuni 3rd, Yoshichika, and Yoshitora. *59 sheets.* (14 × 9¾). **O1. A. 21.**

—— Theatrical Scenes, Portraits of Women and Foreigners, Caricatures, etc.; by Fusatane, Kuniaki, Kunichika (Ichiōsai), Kunisada (Toyokuni 2nd, Kachōrō), Kunisada 2nd, Kunisato (Ryusensai), Kunitsuna, Sadahide (Gountei), Toyokuni, Yoshichika (Ikkeisai), Yoshifuji, Yoshitora, Yoshitoshi (Ikkwaisai), and Yoshitoyo (Ichiryūsai). *228 sheets.* (13¾ × 9½). **O1. A. 22.**

—— Various Traditional and Historical Scenes, Humorous Pictures, Views of noted places in Yedo, etc.; by Hiroshige, Kuniyoshi (Ichiyūsai), Seirei, Yoshimori (Ikkwōsai), Yoshitsuna, and Yoshitsuya (Ichiyeisai). *42 sheets.* (14¼ × 9½). **O1. A. 24.**

—— Battle Scenes, Caricatures, etc.; by Kunitsuna, Kuniyoshi (Ichiyūsai), Ōsai, Sadahide (Gountei), Toyokuni, Yoshichika (Ikkeisai), Yoshifusa (Ippōsai), Yoshimori, Yoshitora (Ichimōsai), Yoshitoshi (Ikkwaisai), and Yoshitsuna (Ittōsai). *51 sheets.* (14 × 10). **O1. A. 28.**

—— Views of noted places (including one of a "Port in the United States"), Humorous Scenes, Children at play, etc.; by Hiroshige, Keisai (Yeisen), Kunisada (Toyokuni 2nd), Kunisada 2nd, Kuniyoshi, Sadatora, Sadayuki, Toyohiro, Toyokuni, Yasuhide, Yoshikazu, and Yoshitora. *90 sheets, in painted cover.* (14½ × 10). **O1. B. 1.**

—— Amusements of the Seasons, Theatrical Scenes, Portraits of Women, Humorous pictures of the great Earthquake in 1855, etc.; by Hiroshige, Kunisada (Toyokuni 2nd), Kunisada 2nd (Baichōrō), Kuniyoshi (Ichiyūsai), Sadahide (Gyokuransai), Shigenobu, and Toyokuni. *50 sheets.* (14½ × 10). **O1. B. 15.**

—— Theatrical Characters, Famous Personages, Humorous, Legendary and other Scenes; by Kunimaro, Kunisada (Toyokuni 2nd, Kachōrō), Kunisada 2nd (Baichōrō), Kuniyoshi (Ichiyūsai, Chōōrō), Toyokuni, and Yoshitoshi (Ikkwaisai). *126 sheets.* (14¼ × 9¾). **O1. B 16.**

ALBUM. — Representations of Types of Female Beauty, Celebrated Personages, Amusements of the Seasons, Theatrical, Fighting and Humorous Scenes, etc.; by Hidekatsu (Isshūsai), Hiroshige (Ichiryūsai), Hōgyoku (*female artist*), Kunimori, Kunisada (Toyokuni 2nd), Kuniteru (Ichiyūsai), Kuniyoshi (Ichiyūsai), Sadahide (Gyokuransai), Shunshō (Kochōyen), Toyokuni, Yoshifuji (Ippōsai), Yoshitora (Ichimōsai), Yoshitsuru (Isseisai), Yoshitsuya (Ichiyeisai), and Yoshiyuki (Ichireisai). *158 sheets.* (14½ × 9¾). **O1. B. 17.**

——— Pictures of famous Heroes, Historical and other Scenes, Humorous Sketches, etc.,; by Kunisada (Toyokuni 2nd), Kuniyoshi, Sadahide (Gountei), Yoshichika (Ikkeisai), Yoshiharu (Ichibaisai), Yoshikazu (Ichijusai), and Yoshitoshi (Ikkwaisai). *62 sheets.* (14¼ × 10). **O1. B. 24.**

——— Theatrical Characters, Portraits of Warriors, Sheet of Caricatures, etc.; by Hirosada, Ichiryōsai, Kunisada (Toyokuni 2nd, Ichiyōsai), Kuniyoshi (Ichiyūsai), Toyokuni, and Yoshitora (Kinchōrō). *57 sheets.* (14½ × 10). **O1. C. 13.**

——— Theatrical Scenes, Portraits, etc.; by Keisai, Kunisada (Toyokuni 2nd), Kuniyoshi, Sadafusa, Yoshimune, and Yoshitsuya, *42 sheets.* (14 × 10). **O2. A. 23.**

——— Theatrical Characters, Picture of the Seven Gods of Good Fortune humorously drawn, etc.; by Baiso (Gengyo), Chikuyōdō, Fujimaru, Fusatane, Gokyōtei, Hiroshige, Ichi-ō Kiku-jo (*female artist*), Kuniaki, Kunichika, Kunisada (Toyokuni 2nd), Kwakuju (Meirindō, *female artist*), Rigyoku, Yoshichika (Ikkeisai), Yoshimori, Yoshitora, Yoshitoshi (Ikkwaisai), and Yoshitsuya (Ichiyeisai). *104 sheets.* (14 × 9½). **O2. A. 25.**

——— Portraits of Women and various Humorous and other Scenes; by Hirosada, Hiroshige, Hokuchō (Shunshosai), Keisai (Yeisen), Kunichika, Kuniharu, Kunisada (Toyokuni 2nd), Kunisada 2nd (Baichōrō), Kuniteru, Kuniyoshi, Shigeharu (Gyokuryūtei), Shigenobu, Toyokuni, Tsukimaro (Bokutei), Yoshichika, and Yoshikazu (Ichijusai). *101 sheets.* (14¼ × 9¾). **O2. A. 26.**

ALBUM.—Theatrical Scenes and Portraits, Caricatures, etc.; by Hiroshige, Kuniyoshi, Sadashige, Toyokuni, Yoshifuji, Yoshitora, and Yoshitsuya. *46 sheets.* (14¼ × 9¾).

O2. A. 22.

——— Theatrical and Humorous Characters; by Kuniyoshi, Tori-jo (*female artist*), and Toyokuni. *89 sheets.* (14¼ × 9¼).

O2. A. 24.

——— Theatrical Portraits, Humorous and other Scenes, etc.; by Hirokage, Hiroshige, Kunisada (Toyokuni 2nd, Ichiyōsai, Kachōrō, Ki-ō, Kokuteisha), Kuniyoshi (Ichiyōsai), Toyokuni (Ichiyōsai, Kachōrō), and Yoshitsuya (Ichiyeisai). *139 sheets.* (14½ × 9½). **O2. B. 27.**

——— Theatrical and other Scenes, Humorous Pictures, etc.; by Kuniyoshi, Toyokuni, Yoshichika, and Yoshitora. *30 sheets.* (14¾ × 10). **O2. B. 28.**

——— Theatrical Scenes, etc.; by Kuniyoshi, Shōjō Kyōsai, and Toyokuni. *30 sheets.* (14½ × 10). **O2. B. 29.**

——— Portraits of Theatrical and other Characters, Various Scenes, etc.; by Chikamaro (Shōjō), Hiroshige (Ichiryūsai), Kunisada 2nd (Baichōrō), Kuniyoshi, Toyokuni, Yoshichika (Ikkeisai), and Yoshitsuya (Ichiyeisai). *141 sheets.* (14½ × 9½). **O2. B. 30.**

——— Theatrical Scenes, Carved figures by Hidari Jingorō, and a copy of Caricatures on a wall; by Kuniyoshi (Ichiyūsai), and Toyokuni. *42 sheets (in 3 portions).* (14½ × 9¾). **O5. C. 20.**

SECTION V*b.*—RELIGION.

HANZAN, Matsugawa.—Nakatomi Ōharai Zuye. A Shintō Prayer, illustrated by Matsugawa Hanzan. *Cuts.* 3 vols. (10 × 7), 1851. **O3. C. 19.**

HIROSHIGE, and KUNISADA (1st and 2nd).—Illustrations to the Thirty-three stories of the Benevolence of the Buddha Kwan-on, with views of Temples, etc., as head-pieces. (1 set complete, by Hiroshige and Kunisada 1st; and 13 of a second series.) *Cuts, col.* (13½ × 9). **O4. G. 1.**

C

Another copy, containing duplicates of the set by Hiroshige and Kunisada 1st ; and 29 of a third series. *Cuts, col.* (13½ × 9). **O4. G. 2.**

KIYOHARU, Hishikawa.—Kwan-on-Kyō Zuye. The Buddhist sacred Book, Kwan-on-Kyō; with illustrations by Hishikawa Kiyoharu. *Cuts.* 3 vols. (10 × 7), 1833.

O3. C. 20.

KōBō Daishi.—Shūko Jisshu. An autograph Treatise on the subject of Buddhism, with seven representations of Buddha; by the priest Kōbō Daishi. *Cuts.* 2 vols. (15 × 10). **O4. B. 2.**

A modern reproduction of a work attributed to Kōbō Daishi (9th cent. A.D.).

MARRIAGE CEREMONY. — Konrei Michi-shirube. Short Account of the Marriage Ceremony. *Cuts, col.* (8 × 6).

O5. D. 41.

SECTION VI.—LANDSCAPE, ARCHITECTURE AND TOPOGRAPHY.

Note.—The ALBUMS classified in Sections VII, and VII*b.*, contain a number of incidental illustrations (exterior and interior) of ARCHITECTURE.

AKISATO Sōseki.—Miyako Meisho Zuye. Historical and traditional Records of the celebrated places of Kyōto and its suburb. Illustrated by Shunchōsai, Takeharo Nobushige, engraved by Nagashima Rokuyemon, compiled by Akisato Sōseki. *Cuts.* 6 vols. (10 × 7) Kyōto, 1780 (9th year of Anyei). **O3. C. 22.**

GAKUTEI, Kyūzan. — Sansui Gwajō. Landscapes. *Cuts, col.* (9 × 6), Nagoya. **O5. E. 27.**

GYOKUYEN, KUNIKAZU, and TōKYO.—Miyako Hyakkei. One hundred Views of Miyako (Kyōto). *50 cuts, col.* (9¼ × 6¾). **O5. C 1.**

HENYEI.—Gentai Gwafu. Text book of Views, Trees, Figures, Buildings, etc., from the Chinese. *Cuts.* 5 vols. (10 × 7) Yedo, 1806. **O5. B. 15.**

HIROSHIGE.—Gojū-san Tsugi. Views (54) of the principal stations in the Tōkaidō. *Cuts, col.* (6½ × 9).

O5. C. 4.

Another Copy (~~with extra plates~~). **O5. C. 5.**

NZAN,Hotta (Horita).- Yehon Konrei michi shirube.
Ill. of the Marriage ceremony. cuts,col. 2 vols.
(8¾x6¼) Kyōto,Bunkwa 1 (A.D. 1804) 08.C.5.

ISATO Ritō.- Settsu meisho dzuye. Guide to the
famous places of Settsu. Compiled by Akisato
Ritō. Ill.by Takehara Shunchōsai (landscapes) &
Niwa Tokei, Ishida Yūtei,Shunsen,Shimogawara Ike
Nakamura Chūka,Nantei & others (figure subjects)
cuts. 12 vols. (10x7½) Kyōto,Kwansei 8 (A.D. 179
08.B.5.

Hiroshige I . good but dirty.
"   "   bad.

HIROSHIGE.—Shodai Hiroshige Meisho. Views of famous
places in Yedo and its suburbs. *Cuts, col.* 2 of a set.
(7 × 5). *See also 04.c.16.* 04. C. 27.

This title is of doubtful authenticity.

HIROSHIGE.—Tōkaidō Gojū-san Tsugi. Views (56) of the Tōkaidō, with Figures. *Cuts, col.* (10 × 7). **O5. C. 2.**

Another copy (with 30 plates). **O5. C. 3.**

—— Views (55) of the Tōkaidō. *Cuts, col.* (13½ × 9). **O4. G. 5.**

—— Views (54) of the Tōkaidō. *Cuts, col., and mounted.* (8¾ × 13¾). **O4. G. 4.**

—— Views (56) of the Tōkaidō. *Cuts, col. and mounted.* (6¼ × 8¼). **O5. A. 6.**

—— Views (51) of the Tōkaidō, and (24) of Noted Places in Yedo. *75 cuts, col.* (8¾ × 6½). **O1. C. 1.**

—— Views (17) of noted places in Yedo. *Cuts, col.* (8¾ × 13½). **O5. C. 7.**

—— Views of noted places in Yedo, and of Mount Fuji from thirty-six different points. *Cuts, col.* (13½ × 8¾). **O4. G. 9.**

—— Yedo Meisho. Views (11) of noted places in Yedo. *Cuts, col.* (7½ × 13). **O5. D. 31.**

—— Yedo Miyage. Views of noted places in Yedo, and its environs. *Cuts, col.* 10 Vols. 1-7, 10. (7 × 5), 1850–67. *see also or. c. 27.* **O4. C. 16.**

—— The Hundred Views of noted places in Yedo. *Cuts, col.* (13½ × 8¾). **O4. G. 10.**

2 other copies, each with additional views. **O4. G. 11, 12.**

—— Shokoku Rokujū Hakkei. Views (68) of the different provinces of Japan. *Cuts, col.* (8¾ × 6½). **O5. D. 30.**

—— Dai Nippon Rokujū-yoshū Meishō Zuye. Views (69) in the provinces of Japan. *Cuts, col.* (13 × 9), 1856. **O5. C. 6.**

—— Views (36) of the Kiso Kaidō. *Cuts, col.* (9 × 13½). **O4. G. 3.**

—— Ōmi Hakkei. The Eight celebrated Views of Lake Biwa. *Cuts, col.* (14 × 9½). **O3. C. 7.**

HIROSHIGE, KUNIYOSHI, and TOYOKUNI.—Views (55) of the Tōkaidō, with supplementary historical, traditional and theatrical pictures. *Cuts, col.* (14½ × 9½). **O4. G. 6.**

Another copy (including 2 not in O4. G. 6).

O4. G. 7.

HOKUSAI.—Fugaku Hyakkei. One Hundred Views of Mount Fuji. *Cuts, tinted.* 3 vols. (9 × 6), 1834.

O5. E. 29.

———— Hokusai Mangwa. Collection of Sketches. *Cuts, col.* 14 vols. (2 copies of vol. 5, 1 with extra cuts). (9 × 6), 1834. **O3. E. 8.**

———— Dōchū Gwafu. Pictures of the Scenery on the Tōkaidō. *Cuts, col.* (9 × 6), 1835. **O5. E. 28.**

HŌSAI.—Kyōchū-no-yama. Landscapes. *Cuts, col.* (10 × 7) Yedo, 1809. **O5. B. 25.**

ICHIRŌ, Yashima.—Ichirō Gwafu. Landscapes. *Cuts, col.* One of a series. (9 × 6). **O5. E. 30.**

KIMURA Tōsen.—Hachiyama Gwafu. Book of Instructions for making Miniature Views of the places along the Tōkaidō. Illustrated by Nan-yūsai Yoshishige. *Cuts, col.* Vol. 3 of a set of 3. (10 × 7), 1848. **O5. C. 8.**

KUNISADA, Kachōrō.—Tōkaidō Gojū-san Tsugi. Views (56) of the Tōkaidō, each with a female Figure in a different style of Dress. *Cuts, col. and mounted.* (10 × 7¼).

O3. F. 1.

KWAIYEN.—Fusō Meisho Zuye. Humorous Verses on noted places in Japan. Compiled by Kwaiyen, illustrated by Seiyō. *Cuts, col.* Vol. 1. (9 × 6), 1836.

O5. E. 31.

KWANGETSU, *Hōkyō.*—Ise Sangū Meisho Zuye. Illustrated and traditional Description of the town of Ise, and the noted places on the way to the Temple (Shintō) of Ise, from Kyōto, for the guidance of travellers. *Cuts.* 5 vols. (the 5th in 2 parts), and a supplement in 2 parts. (11 × 7), 1797. **O5. B. 27.**

MAPS.—Maps of the provinces of Japan. Vol. 2. (7 × 4), 1864. **O4. C. 17.**

HOKUSAI.—Yehon Sumida gawa Riogan Ichiran. Illustrations of both banks of the Sumida river. *Cuts, col.* 3 vols. (11 × 7). **O5. A. 18.**

HOKUSAI.—Yehon Azuma-asobi. Views of noted places in Yedo. Engraved by Andō Yenshi; printed (or written) by Rokuzōtei. *Cuts, col.* 3 vols (11 × 7) Yedo, 1802. **O5. A. 17.**

Impressionist – good copy.

Landscape copied / from Hirsohige 1.

MATSUURA, Takeshirō.—Extracts by Takeshirō Matsuura, from his Diary, and Reports on Geography, Customs, History, Tradition, etc., made to the local Governor of Hakodate, after his journey for this purpose, in 1857; illustrated by different artists. *Cuts, some col.* (10 × 7).

Higashi Yezo Nisshi. Yezo, the Eastern part, now forming part of Hokkaidō. Vols. 1, 2, 4, of a set of 4.
O5. B. 28.

Nishi Yezo Nisshi. Yezo, the Western part, now forming part of Hokkaidō. Vol. 3 of a set of 4.
O5. B. 29.

Nosshafu Nisshi. Nosshafu Nisshi, now forming part of Hokkaidō. 1 vol. of a set of 3. **O5. B. 30.**

Teshi-o Nisshi. Teshi-o Nisshi, now forming part of Hokkaidō. 1 vol. of a set of 5. **O5. B. 31.**

Kusuri Nisshi. Kusuri Nisshi, now forming part of Hokkaidō. 1 vol. of a set of 8. **O5. B. 32.**

Tokachi Nisshi. Tokachi Nisshi, now forming part of Hokkaidō. 1 vol. of a set of 4. **O5. B. 33.**

Yūbari Nisshi. Yūbari Nisshi, now forming part of Hokkaidō. 1 vol. of a set of 4. **O5. B. 34.**

MITSUSADA, *Tosa-no Kami*, etc.—Tōkaidō Meisho Zuye. Historical and Traditional Descriptions of celebrated places on the Tōkaidō. Illustrated by *Tosa-no Kami* Mitsusada, Sansai Soken, Shunsensai, Bummei, Ishida Yūtei, *Hōkyō* Sōyen, Kano Nui-no-suke Nagatoshi, Keisai Masayoshi, and others. *Cuts.* 6 vols. (10 × 7), 1797 **O3. F. 5.**

MURAKAMI.—Banshū Meisho Junran Zuye. Guide book to the province of Harima, with historical and traditional Notes, and illustrations of some Scenes and Views by Rankō. Compiled by Murakami. *Cuts.* 5 vols. (10 × 7), 1803. **O5. C. 9.**

NISHIURA, Sukekata.—Azuma-no Tsuto. Account of the journey from Ôsaka to Yedo and its noted places, in prose and verse. Illustrated by various artists. *Cuts.* 2 vols. (10 × 7), 1812. **O5. C. 10.**

OKADA, Akira, and NOGUCHI, Michinao.—Owari Meisho Zuye. Illustrations of noted places in the province of Owari, with traditional, historical, etc., Notes; compiled by Akira Okada and Michinao Noguchi, illustrated by Shunkō Odagiri. *Cuts.* Parts 5–7 of vol. 1. (11 × 7) Nagoya, 1844 (15th year of Tempō). **O5. B. 35.**

SADANOBU.—Ōmi Hakkei. Eight views along lake Biwa. *Cuts, col. and mounted.* (4¼ × 6½). **O5. C. 5.**

SEI-Ō, Akatsuki.—Yodogawa Ryōgan Ichiran. The Scenery along the banks of the river Yodo, running down to Ōsaka,· through Miyako ; with Accounts of notable places. on it ; illustrated by Matsugawa Hanzan and Hōshunsui. *Cuts, col.* 2 vols. (7 × 5). **O4. C. 18.**

SESSON.—Shūko Jisshu. Two sets, each of eight celebrated Views in China. *Cuts, tinted.* (15 × 10). **O4. B. 3.**
Reproductions of originals dated 1563 A.D.

SHIGENAGA.—Yehon Yedo Miyage. Views of noted places in Yedo, with short stories. Illustrated by Shigenaga. *Cuts.* 3 vols. (9 × 6), 1779. **O5. E. 32.**

SŌYEN, Sakuma, etc.—Miyako Rinsen Meishō Zuye. Historical and Traditional Records of the noted places of Miyako (Kyōto) ; illustrated by Sakuma Sōyen, Nishimura Chūkwa, and Bummei Sadaaki. *Cuts.* 5 vols., (vol. 1 bound in 2). (10 × 7) Kyōto, 1799. **O5. B. 36.**

SUKENOBU, Nishikawa.—Yehon Yamato Hiji. Book of famous Views, noted Personages, etc., with short stories ; illustrated by Nishikawa Sukenobu. *Cuts.* 10 Vols. ~~in a set.~~ (9 × 6) Kyōto, 1716–42. **O5. E. 33.**

TAKENARI, Chikutei.—Tabu ga-mine Nijū-roku Shōshi. Notes and verses of Poetry on the Twenty-six beautiful Scenes in the Tabu mountain ; illustrated by Chikutei Takenari. *Cuts.* (9 × 6) Nara, 1856. **O5. D. 32.**

TANGE, Tsukicka —Tōgoku Meishōshi. Views of noted places in the Eastern part of Japan, with verses of Poetry ; illustrated by Tsukioka Tange, engraved by Yoshimi Niyemon. *Cuts.* 5 vols. (11 × 7), 1762. **O3. F. 2.**

VIEWS.—Nihon Meishō. Celebrated Views in Japan. *Cuts, col.* (6½ × 9¼). **O5. C. 5.**

YEDO.—Landscapes : Famous places in Yedo, with humorous verses. *Cuts.* Vol. 2 of a set of 3. (8 × 6). **O5. D. 33.**

———Views of Noted Places in Yedo, with historical notes. *Cuts, col.* (10 × 7). **O3. F. 3.**

RANKŌ, Nakai, etc.—Itsukushima Zuye. Guide to the temples of Itsukushima, with illustrations of customs, scenery, and historical or legendary accounts of them. Illustrated by Nakai Rankō, Hōyen, and Ōishi Matora. *Cuts.* Vol. 3 of a set. (10 × 7). **O3. F. 18.**

SHUNCHŌSAI, Takehara Nobushige.—Izumi Meisho Zuye. Guide to famous places in the Izumi province with historical and traditional records. *Cuts.* 4 vols. (10 × 7) 1796. **O5. F. 12.**

The complete set of Guides to the Five Provinces, includes also those for the Settsu, Kawachi, Yamashiro and Yamato provinces.

Vols. 6 - 10 . 1742.

SOYEN,Sakuma,etc.- Miyako Rinsen Meishō Zuye. Historical & traditional Records of the noted places of Miyako (Kyōto); Ill. by Sakuma Sōyen, Nishimura Chūkwa,& Bummei Sadaaki. cuts. 1st. series 4 vols. (vol 2 in 2) 1787,2nd. series 5 vols. (vol.1 in 2) 1799. (10x7) Kyōto,1787-99, O3.A.4.

TSURUGA.—Eight views near (?) Tsuruga; with poems. *Cuts, col.* (8 × 9) n.p., n.d. **O4. E. 9.**

This is by Hokusai.   Dup. of 05.

YEDO.—Yedo Meisho Zuye. Views of noted places in Yedo. *Cuts.* Vol. 4. (10 × 7). **O3. F. 4.**

—— Yehon Azuma-asobi. Views of noted places in Yedo. *Cuts, col.* Vol. 3. (10 × 7), 1802. **O5. C. 11.**

YOSHIHARU, Chōkarō.—Miyako Meisho Gwafu. Views of famous places in Miyako (Kyōto). *Cuts, col.* Vol. 1. (7 × 5), 1866. **O4. C. 19.**

YŌYEN, Fujiwara Toshitada, etc.—Zenkwōji Michi Meisho Zuye. Guide book to the noted places in Shinano, for visitors to the Buddhist Temple Zenkwōji; with Historical or Traditional Records. Illustrated by the authors, Yōyen Fujiwara Toshitada, and Haruye Tadachika. *Cuts.* 5 vols. (10 × 7) Nagoya, 1849. **O5. C. 12.**

ALBUMS OF PRINTS IN COLOUR.

ALBUM.—Theatrical Scenes, Portraits of Women, Views and various Scenes; by Hiroshige, Kunisada (Toyokuni 2nd, Gototei), Kunisada 2nd (Baichōrō), Kuniyoshi, Shigenobu, Toyokuni, Yoshikazu, Yoshikuni (Jukōdō), Yoshitora (Ichimōsai), Yoshitsuna, and Yoshitsuya (Ichiyeisai). *49 sheets.* (14¼ × 9¾). **O1. A. 23.**

—— Various Traditional and Historical Scenes, Humorous Pictures, Views of noted places in Yedo, etc.; by Hiroshige, Kuniyoshi (Ichiyūsai), Seirei, Yoshimori (Ikkwōsai), Yoshitsuna, and Yoshitsuya (Ichiyeisai). *42 sheets.* (14¼ × 9½). **O1. A. 24.**

—— Battle Scenes, and a Bird's Eye View of the noted places in the Western Provinces; by Hideteru, Kunichika, Kunihisa, Kunimitsu, Kuniteru, Sadahide, Yoshikazu, Yoshitora, and Yoshitoshi. *41 sheets.* (14½ × 9¾). **O1. A. 29.**

—— Views of noted places (including one of a 'Port in the United States'), Humorous Scenes, Children at play. etc.; by Hiroshige, Keisai (Yeisen), Kunisada (Toyokuni 2nd), Kunisada 2nd, Kuniyoshi, Sadatora, Sadayuki, Toyohiro, Toyokuni, Yasuhide, Yoshikazu, and Yoshitora. *90 sheets, in painted cover.* (14½ × 10). **O1. B. 1.**

ALBUM.—Portraits of Women, Landscapes with figures, etc.; by Hiroshige, Kunisada (Toyokuni 2nd, Kachōrō, Ichiyōsai, Kokuteisha), Kunisada 2nd (Kunimasa, Ichijusai), Shigenobu, Shūchō (Tamagawa), Toyokuni, and Yoshitora (Ichimōsai). *28 sheets.* (14½ × 10).

O1. C. 32.

———— Portraits of Women, Scenes from the novel " Genji Monogatari," Traditional personages, and Landscapes; by Chikamaro, Hiroshige, Keisai (Yeisen), Kunisada 2nd (Baichōrō), Kunitsuna (Ichiransai), Kuniyoshi, Toyokuni, Yoshitoshi (Ikkwaisai), and Yoshitsuya (Ichiyeisai). *98 sheets.* (13 × 9).

O1. D. 11.

———— Pictures of Women in various Scenes, Theatrical Characters, the Ceremony of setting up the framework of a House, etc.; by Keisai (Yeisen), Kunisada (Toyokuni 2nd, Kachōrō), Kuniyasu, Kuniyoshi (Ichiyūsai), Sadafusa (Gokitei), Sadahide, Sadakane, and Toyokuni. *150 sheets.* (14½ × 10).

O1. E. 20.

———— Scenes from the Drama "Chūshingura" (the Story of the Forty-seven Rōnin), Views of noted places in Yedo, etc.; by Hiroshige, Keisai (Yeisen), Kunimaru, Kuninao, Kunitsuna, Shigenobu (Ichiyūsai), and Toyokuni. *88 sheets.* (9½ × 14).

O2. A. 27.

———— Pictures of Beautiful Women, some with quotations from the Hundred Poems, Scenes of the Tamagawa in six different provinces, Theatrical characters, etc.; by Kunisada (Toyokuni 2nd, Kachōrō, Ichiyōsai, Gototei), Kuniyoshi (Ichiyūsai), and Yoshichika. *76 sheets.* (14½ × 10).

O2. B. 31.

———— Theatrical and other Scenes, Portraits of Actors, a View of Yenoshima, etc.; by Hiroshige, Kunisada (Toyokuni 2nd), Kuniyoshi, and Yoshifuji. *56 sheets.* (14¾ × 10).

O2. B. 32.

———— Portraits of Women, and Landscapes; by Gokotei Hiroshige (Ichiryūsai), Keisai (Yeisen), Kunimaru (Ichiyensai), Kuninao, Kunisada (Toyokuni 2nd, Kachōrō, Gototei, Ki-ō), Kunitomi (Kwasentei), Kuniyasu, Kuniyoshi (Ichiyūsai), Sadafusa (Gokitei), Sadahide, Sadatora (Gofūtei), Senchō (Teisai), Shigenobu, Yeizan (Kikugawa), Yoshifuji (Ippōsai), and Yoshitora (Ichimōsai). *100 sheets.* (14 × 9½).

O2. C. 10.

Kuniyoshi (Ichiyūsai)

02. A. 27. Transferred to Print Collection

Kunifuku.
Tsuyanaga.

ALBUM.—Landscapes, and Illustrations of Warriors; by
Hiroshige, Keisai (Yeisen), and Kuniyoshi. *13 sheets.*
(10 × 14). **O4. F. 4.**

———— Portraits of Women, Theatrical Scenes, Views, etc. ;
by Hiroshige, Kunisada (Toyokuni 2nd), Kunisada 2nd,
Kuniyoshi, Toyokuni, and Yoshifuji. *69 sheets.*
(10 × 12¾). **O4. F. 6.**

———— Views of the Tōkaidō; by Chikamaro, Hiroshige,
Kunichika, Kunisada, Kunitsuna, Kuniyoshi, Sadahide,
Toyokuni, Yenchō, Yoshichika, Yoshikata, Yoshimori,
Yoshimune, Yoshitora, Yoshitoshi, and Yoshitsuya. *162
sheets.* (14 × 9½). **O4. G. 8.**

———— Views of Noted Places in Yedo, various Provinces,
and Nikkō; by Hiroshige, Sadanobu, and Yeisen. *34
sheets.* (9½ × 13¼). **O5. C. 13.**

SECTION VII.—COSTUME (GENERAL COLLECTIONS).

AKATSUKI Kanenari.—Kompira Sankei Meisho Zuye.
Guide book with historical and traditional Records for
visitors to the Shintō temple, Kompira, in the province
of Sanuki. Illustrated by Urakawa Kinsuke. *Cuts.*
6 vols. (10 × 7), 1847. **O3. C. 21.**

AMUSEMENTS.—Amusements of the Seasons. *Cuts.* (9 × 6).
O5. D. 35.

———— Yehon Shiki-no-asobi. Amusements of the Seasons,
wit verses c poetry. *Cuts.* (9 × 6). **O5. D. 34.**

CHIKANOBU, Yōshū, and HŌSAI.—Imayō Genji. Scenes
fr the novel " Genji Monogatari ; " with modern
characters from paintings by Hōsai, and Yōshū Chikanobu. 2 vols. (7 × 5) **O4. E. 8.**

CHILDREN.—Yehon Yamato Warambe. Pictures of Children
at Play, Warriors, etc. *Cuts.* 3 vols. in 2. (9 × 6).
O5. D. 36.

COSTUMES.—Two hundred patterns of Ladies' Dresses.
Cuts. Vol. 2 of a set. (7 × 5), 1667. **O4. C. 20.**

CUSTOMS.—Illustrations of Customs. *Cuts.* (9 × 6).
O5. D. 45.

ETIQUETTE.—Etiquette; Stories of noted Women with
poems relating to them; selected Poems with Portraits
of the authors; and various useful information for
Ladies. *Cuts.* (10 × 7) Ōsaka, 1811. **O3. F. 6.**

ETIQUETTE —Etiquette for Ladies. *Cuts.* (10 × 7).
O5. C. 14.

———— Musume Kyōkun Waka Hyakushu. Moral lessons and Etiquette for young Ladies, in one hundred verses of poetry with explanation. *Cuts.* (10 × 7). **O5. C. 15.**

HASEGAWA. — Hana-fubuki. Illustrations of the Course of Life, with moral lessons; illustrated by Hasegawa. *Cuts.* 1 vol. of a set of 3. (9 × 6). **O5. D. 37.**

HENYEI.—Gentai Gwafu. Text book of Views, Trees, Figures, Buildings, etc., from the Chinese. *Cuts.* 5 vols. (10 × 7) Yedo, 1806. **O5. B. 15.**

HIROSHIGE.—Tōkaidō Gojū-san Tsugi. Views (56) of the Tōkaidō, with Figures. *Cuts, col.* (10 × 7). **O5. C. 2.**

Another copy (with 30 plates). **O5. C. 3.**

HIROSHIGE, KUNIYOSHI, and TOYOKUNI.—Portraits of noted historical, traditional and theatrical Personages, each with a short Biography, and one of the Hundred Poems. *Cuts, col.* (13½ × 8¾). **O4. G. 13.**

HOKKEI.—Hokuri Jūniji. Story, with illustrations of various Domestic and Street Scenes. *Cuts.* (11 × 7) Yedo. **O3. F. 7.**

HOKUSAI.—Hokusai Mangwa. Collection of Sketches. *Cuts, col.* 14 vols. (2 copies of vol. 5, 1 with extra cuts). (9 × 6), 1834. **O3. E. 8.**

———— Hokusai Gwafu. Pictures of Figures, Landscapes, Birds, Flowers, etc. 2 ed. *Cuts, col.* Vols. 1, 2. (9 × 6) Nagoya, 1875. **O3. E. 10.**

HOKUSAI, Kōkei.—Kyōka Gojūnin Isshu. Fifty verses of humorous Poetry by different authors, with their portraits; illustrated by Kōkei Hokusai. *Cuts.* (10 × 7), 1819. **O3. F. 8.**

KISEKI.—Yehon Tatoye-gusa. Witty Phrases; illustrated by Nishikawa Sukenobu. *Cuts.* 3 vols. (9 × 6), 1731. **O5. D. 39.**

———— Onna Fūzoku Tamakagami. Etiquette for Ladies. Illustrated by Nishikawa Sukenobu. *Cuts.* 2 vols. (9 × 6) Kyōto, 1782. **O5. D. 38.**

HOMMA Yoichi (?).—Fukushoku Zukai. Ceremonial uni-
form for courtiers, with detailed illustration of the
various garments, etc., by Yokokawa Shigetaka. Compiled by Homma Yoichi of Ichinoseki in Ōshū, for private
circulation. *Cuts, col.* (11 × 8) 1816. **O5. A. 15.**

MASANOBU,Kitao.- Seiro Meikun **Jihitsushu**. Patterns of
the autographs of famous courtesans. Portraits of
14 famous ladies of the Yoshiwara,each with a
poem written by herself. cuts,col. (15x10) Yedo,
1783.   publisher: Tsutaya.   04.8.10.

NANBOKU,Aoki.- Saishiki kokonoye Nishiki. Patterns o
Japanese ladies dresses. Engraved & published by
Nakazawa Kōseido. cuts,col. Vol 1 of 2. (11x7$\frac{3}{4}$)
Ōsaka,Tennei 4,12th. month (A.D. 1784) 08.8.1.

NANKATEI.- Hinagata tsugiko zakura. Patterns of
dresses compiled by Nankatei. cuts.(9$\frac{3}{4}$x6$\frac{3}{4}$) Iyo
Matsuyama, Hōreki 8 (A.D. 1758)   08.8.14.

KITAO.—Yehon Azuma Karage. Drawings of noted places of resort in Yedo, with humorous verses. *Cuts.* 3 vols. (9 × 6). **O5. D. 40.**

KODERA Kiyoyuki.—Bitchū Meishō-kō. Illustrated account of noted places in the province of Bitchū. Illustrated by Tsuji Hozan. *Cuts, tinted.* 2 vols. (11 × 7) Ōsaka, 1822. **O5. B. 26.**

KUNISADA 2nd, Baichōrō.—Fifty-four scenes from the novel "Genji Monogatari." *Cuts, col.* (13 × 9¼). **O5. C. 16.**

KUNISADA, Kachōrō.—Tōkaidō Gojū-san Tsugi. Views (56) of the Tōkaidō, each with a female Figure in a different style of Dress. *Cuts, col. and mounted.* (10 × 7½). **O3. F. 1.**

KUNIYOSHI, Ichiyūsai, and YOSHIKAZU, Ichijusai.—Portraits of famous historical Personages, with verses of poetry. *Cuts, col.* (14½ × 9¾). **O4. G. 14.**

KYŌDEN, Seisei Rōjin, *pseud.*—Kottō-shū. Information on various subjects ; compiled by Seisei Rōjin (Kyōden). *Cuts.* Vol. 1, part 1 and portion of part 2. (10 × 7), 1804. **O3. F. 9.**

MARRIAGE CEREMONY.—Konrei Michi-shirube. Short Account of the Marriage Ceremony. *Cuts, col.* (8 × 6). **O5. D. 41.**

MORAL LESSONS.—Onna Shisho Zuye. The four Chinese Books of Moral Lessons for Ladies ; Jokai, Onna Kōkyō, Onna Rongo, and Koji Retsujo-den. With illustrated stories. *Cuts and borders, some col.* 4 vols. (10 × 7), 1835. **O5. C. 17.**

MORAL STORIES.—Onna Kakun. Moral Stories for Women. *Cuts.* Vols. 1, 2, of a set of 3. (9 × 6), 1729. **O5. D. 42.**

MORALS.—Book of Morals. *Cuts.* (8 × 6). **O5. D. 43.**

POEMS.—Sugataye. One hundred verses of Poetry. *Cuts.* Vol. 3. (9 × 6). **O5 ~~O4~~. D. 15.**

———— Yehon Chitose-yama. Poems and Moral Lessons. Pages 9–13 of vol. 2 bound with vol. 3, of a set of 3. *Cuts.* (9 × 6). **O5. D. 18.**

———— Yehon Mina-no-gawa. Verses from famous Poems. *Cuts.* Vol. 1 and first part of vol. 2 bound together, of a set of 3. (9 × 6). **O5. D. 21.**

Rokujuyen.—Poems by different authors. Compiled by Rokujuyen. *Cuts.* (9 × 6). **O5. D. 27.**

Scenes.—Compilation of fragments of Scenes, etc. *Cuts, col.* (7 × 5). **O4. C. 21.**

———— Yehon Kunimi-yama. Scenes in Foreign Countries. *Cuts.* Vol. 1 of a set of 2 or 3. (9 × 6). **O5. D. 44.**

Shōba.—Yehon Shiki-no-asobi. Amusements of the Seasons, with humorous verses of Poetry. Illustrated by Shōba. *Cuts.* (7 × 5). **O4. C. 22.**

Shūsui, Shimokōbe.—Iroha-uta Yeshō. Verses of Poetry on moral subjects for Children; illustrated by Shimokōbe Shūsui. *Cuts.* 3 vols. in 1. (9 × 6), 1775. **O5. E. 4.**

Sukenobu, Nishikawa, Bunkwado. — Amusements of Women. *Cuts.* (9 × 6), 1736. **O5. D. 45.**

———— Hyakunin Jorō Shinasadame. Pictures of women. *Cuts.* Vol. 2. (11 × 8), 1723. **O3. F. 10.**

-———— Zoku Hyakushu. Verses of moral Poetry; illustrated by Nishikawa Sukenobu. *Cuts.* Vol. 3 of a set of 3. (9 × 6), 1739. **O5. E. 9.**

Tanekiyo.—Suiko Gwaden. Short lives of the Hundred and Eight Heroes from the Chinese novel "Suikoden;" composed by Tanekiyo, illustrated by Hokkei. *Cuts, col.* 3 vols. (9 × 6), 1856. **O5. E. 21.**

Kunisada.
~~Toyokuni.~~ — Fifty-four scenes from the novel "Genji Monogatari." *Cuts, col. and mounted.* (10 × 7). **O5. A. 7.**

———— Hana-kurabe (Comparison of Flowers). Illustrations of noted and legendary Characters. *91 cuts, col.* (15 × 10). **O3. G. 2.**

-———- Illustrations of noted Characters, some with Poems. *73 cuts, col.* (15 × 10). **O3. G. 1.**

~~Toyokuni, Kachōrō, Kokuteisha, Ichiyōsai.~~—Sono Sugata, Yukari-no Utsushi-ye. Fifty-four Scenes from the novel "Genji Monogatari." *Cuts, col.* (9½ × 14). **O4. G. 15.**

? are the other two bound with this parts of same publication.

IKEN.- Hinagata Yoshino-Yama (Pattern of Yoshino ountain) Ancient patterns of Dresses; compiled by ōseiken,engraved by Kikuya Kihei. Designs by Matudaya Hikohichi (vol 1.) Yebishiya Tadahichi of yōto & Sasaya Jingorō of Iyo,Uwajima (vol 11); onomura Chubei of Kyōto,Matsudaya Hokohichi of Iyo atsuyama,Yanagiya of Iyo,Ozaki Useki of Ise Shiriko, Yoshidaya of Iyo Matsuyama. cuts. 3 vols.($10\frac{1}{4}$x$7\frac{1}{2}$) yōto,Meiwa 2,1st month,(A.D. 1765)   08.8.6.

Kunisada.

AMAGUCHI,Soken.- Yamatojin butsu gwafu. Ill. of different classes of Japanese people. cuts. 3 vols. ($10\frac{1}{2}$x7) Kyōto,Bunkwa 1,11th.Month. (A.D. 1804)   08.8.7.

YEITAKU, Sensai.—Onko Nenjū Giōji. Collection of ordi-
nary events during the year. *Cuts.* Vol. 1 (for
January and February), of a set. (9 × 6) Tôkyô, 18`3.
O3. E. 27.

Broken Up.

Tsukioka (? Settei).—Sho-rei-kun. Book of Etiquette.
Illustrated by Tsukioka. *Cuts.* 3 vols. (9 × 6).

O5. D. 46.

ALBUMS OF PRINTS IN COLOUR.

Note.—These ALBUMS will be found valuable for the study
of all details of JAPANESE DOMESTIC LIFE, as well as
that of COSTUME.

ALBUM.—Theatrical Scenes, Portraits of Women, Amuse-
ments of the Seasons, etc.; by Hiroshige, Kunichika,
Kunihisa, Kunisada 2nd, Kunitsuna, Kuniyoshi, and
Toyokuni. *76 sheets.* (14¼ × 10). O1. A. 1.

———— Scenes from the Life of Prince Genji, from the novel
"Genji Monogatari," Amusements of the Seasons, etc.;
by Hiroshige (Ryūsai), Keisai (Yei-en), Kunichika
(Kaseisha), Kunihisa, Kunisada (Toyokuni 2nd),
Kunisada 2nd (Baichōrō), Kunitaka (Ichigyokusai),
Kuniyoshi, Shigenobu, Toyokuni, and Yoshitora
(Kinchōrō). *96 sheets.* (14 × 10¼). O1. A. 2.

———— Portraits of Noted Personages with short Stories;
by Hiroshige, Kunihisa, Kunisada (Toyokuni 2nd),
Kuniyoshi, and Yoshitoshi. *39 sheets.* (14¼ × 10).

O1. A. 3.

———— Portraits, Wrestlers, and various Scenes; by Kunisada (Toyokuni 2nd), Kuniyoshi, Sadahide, Yoshitora,
and Yoshitoshi. *24 sheets.* (13¾ × 10). O1. A. 4.

———— Various Scenes; by Hiroshige, Kunisada (Toyokuni 2nd), Kunisada 2nd, Kuniyoshi, and Yoshitoshi.
32 sheets. (14 × 9½). O1. A. 5.

———— Various Scenes; by Hirokage, Kunitsuna, and
Kuniyoshi. *28 sheets.* (14¼ × 9¾). O1. A. 6.

———— Amusements of Nobles, from the "Genji Monogatari"; by Kunisada (Toyokuni 2nd), Kunisada 2nd
(Baichōrō), Kuniyoshi (Ichiyūsai), and Toyokuni. *76
sheets.* (14¼ × 10). O1. A. 7.

———— Amusements of the Seasons, Portraits of Women,
etc.; by Hiroshige, Kunisada 2nd (Baichōrō), Kuniteru (Ichiyūsai), Kuniyoshi, Sadahide (Gyokuransai),
Shigenobu, and Toyokuni. *54 sheets.* (14¼ × 9¾)

O1. A. 8.

ALBUM.—Portraits of Women, Theatrical Characters, Warriors, Wrestlers, Playing Cards, etc.; by Hiroshige, Keisai (Yeisen), Kuniaki, Kunisada (Toyokuni 2nd, Kachōrō), Kuniteru (Ichiyōsai), Kuniyoshi (Ichiyūsai), Sadahide, Toyokuni (Gosotei), Yoshifuji, Yoshikatsu (Isseisai), Yoshikazu, and Yoshitora. *43 sheets.* (14 × 9)

O1. A. 9.

———— Portraits of Women, Theatrical Scenes, Amusements of the Seasons, etc.; by Fusatane, Kunichika, Kuniharu, Kunisada (Toyokuni 2nd), Kunisada 2nd (Baichōrō), Kuniteru, Kuniyoshi, Osai, Sadahide, Shigenobu, Toyokuni, Yoshichika, and Yoshitoshi. *100 sheets.* (14 × 9¾).

O1. A. 10.

———— Azuma Nishikiye. Pictures printed at Yedo; Various Characters. By Fusatane (Isshōsai), Hiroshige, Ichiyōsai, Kuniaki, Kunichika (Ōsai), Kunisada (Toyokuni 2nd), Kunitsuna, Toyokuni (Ki-ō), Yoshichika (Chōkarō, Ikkeisai), Yoshitora, and Yoshitoshi (Ikkwaisai). *99 sheets.* (14 × 10).

O1. A. 11.

———— Theatrical and other Characters, Amusements of the Seasons, etc.; by Fusatane, Hirosada, Hiroshige, Kuniaki, Kunichika, Kunimasu, Kunimichi, Kunimura, Kunisada (Toyokuni 2nd), Kunisada 2nd (Baichōrō), Kunisato, Kuniteru (Ichiyūsai), Kunitsuna, Kuniyuki, Sadahide (Gyokuran), Sadakage (Gokotei), Sadatora, Sadatoshi, Sadayuki, Toyokuni, and Yoshichika (Chōkarō). *86 sheets.* (14½ × 10).

O1. A. 12.

———— Humorous Pictures and various Scenes with Wrestlers, Acrobats, Warriors, etc.; by Hirokage, Hiroshige, Joshū, Kunisada 2nd (Baichōrō), Kuniyoshi, Kyōsai, Sadahide (Gountei), Toyokuni, Yoshichika (Ikkeisai), Yoshiharu (Ichibaisai), Yoshimasa (Ippōsai), Yoshimori (Ikkwōsai), and Yoshitora. *71 sheets.* (14 × 9¾).

O1. A. 13.

———— Amusements of the Seasons and of Prince Genji, Theatrical Scenes, etc.; by Hiroshige, Kunisada (Toyokuni 2nd), Kunisada 2nd, Kunisato, and Toyokuni. *168 sheets.* (14 × 9¾).

O1. A. 14.

———— Theatrical Scenes and Characters, Chinese Heroes from the novel "Suikoden," and various scenes; by Hiroshige, Hokushū (Shunkōsai), Kunihisa, Kunisada 2nd (Baichōrō), Kunisato, Kuniyoshi, Toyokuni, Yoshiharu (Ichibaisai), and Yoshitora (Kinchōrō). *38 sheets.* (14½ × 10).

O1. A. 15.

ALBUM.—Pictures of various Ceremonies, Processions, Military and Dramatic Scenes ; by Hiroshige, Kunimasa, Kunisada (Toyokuni 2nd), Kunisada 2nd, Kuniteru, Kuniyoshi, Sadahide, Sadashige, Yoshitora, and Yoshitsuya. *141 sheets.* (14¼ × 10). **Ol. A. 16.**

—— Amusements of the Seasons with figures of Women for the most part taken from the novel "Genji Monogatari"; by Hiroshige, Kunichika (Kwachōrō, Ichiōsai), Kunisada (Toyokuni 2nd, Gototei), Kunisada 2nd (Baichōrō), Kuniteru (Ichiyūsai), Toyokuni, and Yoshitora (Kinchōrō). *101 sheets.* (14¼ × 10). **Ol. A. 17.**

—— Amusements of Ladies, Theatrical Characters, etc. ; by Hiroshige, Kunisada (Toyokuni 2nd, Kachōrō), Kuniyoshi (Ichiyūsai), Yoshitora (Ichimōsai), and Yoshiume. *28 sheets.* (14 × 10). **Ol. A. 18.**

—— Amusements of the Seasons, Theatrical Characters and Scenes, etc. ; by Hiroshige, Kunisada (Toyokuni 2nd), Kunisada 2nd, Kuniteru, Kuniyoshi, and Toyokuni. *106 sheets.* (14¼ × 9¾). **Ol. A. 19.**

—— Pictures of various Amusements of the Seasons ; by Chikanobu, Hiroshige, Kuniaki, Kunichika, Kunisada (Toyokuni 2nd), Kunisada 2nd (Baichōrō), Kuniyoshi, Sadahide, Toyokuni, and Yoshitora. *55 sheets.* (14¼ × 9½). **Ol. A. 20.**

—— Scenes from the Life of Prince Genji, Views of noted places in Yedo, some with comic accidents, Scenes showing the influence of Good and Evil Spirits upon two youths, etc. ; by Hiroshige, Kazukage (Shōsai), Kiku-o, Kunichika, Kunimasa, Toyokuni 3rd, Yoshichika, and Yoshitora. *59 sheets.* (14 × 9¾). **Ol. A. 21.**

—— Theatrical Scenes, Portraits of Women and Foreigners, Caricatures, etc. ; by Fusatane, Kuniaki, Kunichika (Ichiōsai), Kunisada (Toyokuni 2nd, Kachōrō) Kunisada 2nd, Kunisato (Ryūsensai), Kunitsuna, Sadahide (Gountei), Toyokuni, Yoshichika (Ikkeisai), Yoshifuji, Yoshitora, Yoshitoshi (Ikkwaisai), and Yoshitoyo (Ichiryūsai). *228 sheets.* (13¾ × 9½). **Ol. A. 22.**

48

ALBUM.—Theatrical Scenes. Portraits of Women, Views and various Scenes; by Hiroshige, Kunisada (Toyokuni 2nd, Gototei). Kunisada 2nd (Baichōrō), Kuniyoshi, Shigenobu, Toyokuni, Yoshikazu, Yoshikuni (Jukōdō), Yoshitora (Ichimōsai), **Yoshitsuna**, and Yoshitsuya (Ichiyeisai). *49 sheets.* (14¼ × 9¾). **Ol. A. 23.**

—— Various Traditional and Historical Scenes, Humorous Pictures, Views of noted places in Yedo, etc.; by Hiroshige, Kuniyoshi (Ichiyūsai), Seirei, Yoshimori (Ikkwōsai), Yoshitsuna, and Yoshitsuya (Ichiyeisai). *42 sheets.* (14¼ × 9½). **Ol. A. 24.**

TOYOKUNI, Kachōrō, Ichiyōsai.—Scenes, with poems, from the novel "Genji Monogatari." *52 sheets.* (10 × 7¼). **Ol. B. 2.**

ALBUM.—Portraits of Women, and Amusement Scenes; by Hiroshige, Kuniaki, Kunisada (Toyokuni 2nd, Kachōrō), Kunisada 2nd (Baichōrō), Kūniteru, Toyokuni, and Yoshichika (Ikkeisai). *66 sheets.* (14½ × 10). **Ol. B. 3.**

—— Portraits of Women and various Scenes; by Kunisada (Toyokuni 2nd), Kunisada 2nd (Baichōrō), Kuniyoshi (Ichiyūsai), Toyokuni, and Yoshichika (Ikkeisai). *19 sheets.* (14½ × 10). **Ol. B. 4.**

—— Historical and Legendary Scenes, etc.; by Kiyomine, Kunisada (Toyokuni 2nd), Kuniyoshi, Shuntei, Toyokuni, and Yoshichika. *48 sheets.* (14½ × 10). **Ol. B. 5.**

—— Battle and other Scenes, Portraits of Poets, etc.; by Kunisada (Toyokuni 2nd), Kunisada 2nd, Kuniyoshi, Sadahide, Toyokuni, Yenrōsai, and Yoshitsuya. *60 sheets.* (14½ × 10). **Ol. B. 6.**

—— Amusements and Theatrical Scenes, Views, etc.; by Beikwa, Hiroshige, Keisai (Yeisen), Kumezō, Kunihisa, Kunisada (Toyokuni 2nd, Gototei), Kunisada 2nd, Kuniyoshi, Muga, and Toyokuni. *72 sheets.* (14½ × 9½). **Ol. B. 7.**

—— Portraits of Women and Amusements of the Seasons; by Hiroshige, Kunitsuna, and Toyokuni. *97 sheets.* (14½ × 10). **Ol. B. 8.**

Transferred to Catalogue, part II
J 5015 – 5034.

ALBUM.—Scenes of various Amusements; by Kunihiko, Kunisada (Toyokuni 2nd), Kunisada 2nd (Baichōrō), **Kuniteru** (Ichiyūsai), Kuniyoshi (Ichiyūsai), and **Toyokuni.** *100 sheets.* (14¼ × 9¾). **Ol. B. 9.**

—— Pictures of Children, etc. ; by Hiroshige, Keisai (Yeisen), Kunisada (Toyokuni 2nd), Kuniyoshi, Sadahide (Gountei), Sadatora, Toyokuni, and Yoshitora (Ichimōsai). *36 sheets.* (14¼ × 10). **Ol. B. 10.**

—— Scenes from the novel "Genji Monogatari," Portraits, Theatrical Scenes, etc. ; by Hiroshige, Kunisada (Toyokuni 2nd), Kuniyoshi, Sadamasa, Toyokuni, and Yoshifuji. *44 sheets.* (14½ × 10). **Ol. B. 11.**

—— Representations of various Amusements and Ceremonies, Theatrical Scenes, etc.; by Kuniteru, Kuniyoshi, Toyokuni, and Yoshifuji. *136 sheets.* (15 × 9¾). **Ol. B. 12.**

—— Theatrical, Historical and other Scenes; by Hiroshige (Ichiryūsai), Hokuju (Shunshōsai), Hokushū (Shunkōsai), Hokuyei (Shunkōsai), Keisai (Yeisen), Kiyoharu (Hishikawa), Kuninao (Utagawa), Kunisada (Toyokuni 2nd, Gototei, Kachōrō), Kuniyoshi (Ichiyūsai), Sadahide (Gountei), Sadamasu (Utagawa), Sadanobu (Hasegawa), and Shigeharu (Ryūsai). *99 sheets.* (15 × 10¼). **Ol. B. 13.**

—— Theatrical Characters, Views of noted Places in Yedo, Popular and Historical Scenes ; by Ashiyuki (Kegwadō), Hikokuni, Hiroshige, Hokuju (Shunshosai), Hokushū (Shunkōsai), Hokuyei (Shumbaisai), Kunimaro (Ichiyensai), Kunisada (Toyokuni 2nd, Gototei), Kuniyoshi (Ichiyūsai), Sadahiro (Gochōtei), Sadamasu (Hasegawa), Sadanobu (Hasegawa), Shibakuni (Saikwōtei), Yoshifuji (Ippōsai), Yoshikuni (Jukōdō), and Yoshitora (Ichimōsai). *139 sheets.* (14¾ × 10¾). **Ol. B. 14.**

—— Amusements of the Seasons, Theatrical Scenes, Portraits of Women. Humorous pictures of the great Earthquake in 1855, etc. ; by Hiroshige, Kunisada (Toyokuni 2nd), Kunisada 2nd (Baichōrō), **Kuniyoshi** (Ichiyūsai), Sadahide (Gyokuransai), Shigenobu, and Toyokuni. *50 sheets.* (14½ × 10). **Ol. B. 15.**

o 75435. D

ALBUM.—Theatrical Characters, Famous personages, Humorous, Legendary and other Scenes; by Kunimaro, Kunisada (Toyokuni 2nd, Kachōrō), Kunisada 2ud (Baichōrō), Kuniyoshi (Ichiyūsai Chōōrō), Toyokuni, and Yoshitoshi (Ikkwaisai). *126 sheets.* (14¼ × 9¾). **Ol. B. 16.**

———— Representations of Types of Female Beauty, Celebrated personages. Amusements of the Seasons, Theatrical, Fighting and Humorous Scenes, etc.; by Hideyoshikatsu (Isshūsai), Hiroshige (Ichiryūsai), Hōgyoku(*female artist*), Kunimori, Kunisada (Toyokuni 2nd), Kuniteru (Ichiyūsai), Kuniyoshi (Ichiyūsai), Sadahide (Gyokuransai), Shunshō (Kochōyen), Toyokuni, Yoshifuji (Ippōsai), Yoshitora (Ichimōsai), Yoshitsuru (Isseisai), Yoshitsuya (Ichiyeisai), and Yoshiyuki (Ichireisai). *158 sheets.* (14½ × 9¾). **Ol. B. 17.**

———— Amusements of the Seasons, Pictures of Women and Warriors, etc.; by Kunimaro (Ichiyensai), Kuniteru (Ichiyūsai), Kuniyoshi (Ichiyūsai), Toyokuni, and Yoshifuji (Ippōsai). *102 sheets.* (14½ × 10½). **Ol. B. 18.**

———— Portraits of Women, and Historical Scenes (including a set of portraits of Mikado); by Chikanobu (Yōshūsai), Hiroshige, Kunichika (Toyohara), Kunihisa (Ichiryūsai), Kunihisa (Ippōsai), Kunisada (Toyokuni 2nd), Kunisada 2nd, Kuniyoshi (Ichiyūsai), Sadanobu (Hasegawa), Senchō (Sogetsuyen), Toyokuni, and Yoshitoshi (Ōso). *38 sheets.* (14¼ × 10). **Ol. B. 19.**

———— Portraits of Women and Warriors, Theatrical, Battle, and other Scenes, etc.; by Hiroshige, Kunisada (Toyokuni 2nd), Kuniyasu, Toyohiro, and Toyokuni. *89 sheets.* (14½ × 10). **Ol. B. 20.**

———— Portraits of Women, Theatrical Scenes and various Views; by Hiroshige (Ichiryūsai), Kunisada (Toyokuni 2nd, Ichiyōsai, Kachōrō), Kuniyoshi (Ichiyūsai), Sadafusa, and Toyokuni. *101 sheets.* (14½ × 10). **Ol. C. 2.**

———— Theatrical, Historical and other Scenes, Views, Portraits of Women, etc.; by Hiroshige, Keisai (Yeisen), Kunichika, Kunihisa, Kunisada (Toyokuni 2nd), Kunisada 2nd, Kuniteru, Kunitsuna, Kuniyoshi, Sadahide, Toyokuni, Yoshichika, Yoshikazu, and Yoshitoshi. *105 sheets.* (14½ × 10). **Ol. C. 3.**

Yoshitama (Ichijōai)

ALBUM.—Portraits of Women and Notabilities, Theatrical and street scenes, etc.; by Hiroshige (Ichiryūsai), Keisai (Yeisen), Kunisada (Toyokuni 2nd, Kachōrō), Kunisada 2nd (Baichōrō), Kunisato, Kuniteru (Ichiyūsai), Kuniyasu, Kuniyoshi (Ichiyūsai), Sadahide (Gountei), Shigenobu (Ichiyūsai), Shunshō (Kochōyen), Toyokuni, Yoshinobu (Ichiyōsai), and Yoshitora (Kinchōrō). *80 sheets.* (14 × 9¼).   O1. C. 4.

——— Illustrations to the Hundred Poems, Scenes from the Life of the Soga Brothers, the novel "Genji Monogatari," etc.; by Hiroshige, Kunisada (Toyokuni 2nd), Kuniyoshi, Sadakage (Gokotei), and Shōjō Kyōsai. *77 sheets.* (14¾ × 10).   O1. C. 5.

——— Portraits of Famous Personages with quotations from the Hundred Poems, Amusements of the Seasons, etc.; by Hiroshige, Kunimori (Ippōsai), Kunisada (Toyokuni 2nd), Kuniyoshi, Shigeharu (Ryūsai), and Toyokuni. *103 sheets.* (14½ × 10).   O1. C. 6.

——— Pictures of various Amusements, Theatrical and Legendary Scenes, Portraits of Women, etc.; by Hiroshige (Ichiryūsai), Kunisada (Toyokuni 2nd, Kachōrō, Ichiyōsai, Kokuteisha, Gototei), Kunisada 2nd (Ichijusai, Baichōrō), Kuniteru, Kuniyoshi (Ichiyūsai), Toyokuni, Toyoshige, and Yeizan. *58 sheets.* (14 × 10).   O1. C. 7.

——— Portraits of Women, Country Scenes, etc.; by Keisai (Yeisen, Ippitsuan), Kunikane (Ippōsai), Kunisada (Toyokuni 2nd, Gototei), Sadatora (Gofūtei), Senchō (Sogetsuan), Shōgetsu (Suiyōtei), Shunsen (Kachōsai), Toyohiro, Toyokuni, Tsukimaro, Utamaro, and Yeizan (Kikugawa). *50 sheets.* (14 × 9).   O1. C. 8.

——— Theatrical and Historical Scenes, etc.; by Hiroshige, Keisai (Yeisen), Kunisada (Toyokuni 2nd), Kuniyoshi, Yoshitora, and Yoshitsuya. *28 sheets.* (14½ × 10).
                                                                    O1. C. 9.

——— Portraits of Women, Theatrical Characters, Amusements of the Seasons, and a Procession of Loo Choo Islanders; by Hokuyei (Shunkōsai, Shumbaisai), Keisai (Yeisen), Kunihiro, Kunisada (Toyokuni 2nd, Kokuteisha, Ichiyōsai, Gototei, Kachōrō), Kuniyasu (Ippōsai), Kuniyoshi (Ichiyūsai), Sadakage (Gokotei), Senchō (Teisai), Shigeharu (Gyokuryūtei), Toyokuni, and Yeizan. *60 sheets.* (14½ × 10).   O1. C. 10.

ALBUM.—Portraits of Women, Amusements of the Seasons, etc.; by Hiroshige, Kuniaki, Kunisada (Toyokuni 2nd), Kunisada 2nd (Baichōrō), Kuniteru, Kuniyasu (Ippōsai), Kuniyoshi, and Toyokuni. *74 sheets.* (14 × 9½).
O1. C. 11.

————— Theatrical, Battle, and other Scenes, Portraits of Women, etc.; by Hiroshige, Kunisada (Toyokuni 2nd), Kuniyoshi, Toyokuni, Yoshichika, and Yoshitora. *37 sheets.* (14½ × 10).
O1. C. 12.

————— Theatrical Characters, Portraits of Warriors, Sheet of Caricatures, etc.; by Hirosada, Ichiryōsai, Kunisada (Toyokuni 2nd, Ichiyōsai), Kuniyoshi (Ichiyūsai), Toyokuni, and Yoshitora (Kinchōrō). *57 sheets.* (14½ × 10).
O1. C. 13.

————— Theatrical Scenes, Portraits of Women, Illustrations of Lyrical Odes, etc.; by Ashiyuki (Kegwadō) Hiroshige, Hokuyei (Shumbaisai, Shunkōsai), Kunisada (Toyokuni 2nd, Gototei, Kachōrō), Kunisato, Kuniyasu, Kuniyoshi (Ichiyūsai, Chōōrō), Sadatora (Gofūtei), Shigeharu (Gyokuryūtei), Toyokuni, Yeizan (Kikugawa), Yoshikazu (Ichijusai), and Yoshitsuya (Ichiyeisai). *60 sheets.* (14¼ × 9¾).
O1. D. 1.

————— Amusements of the Seasons, etc.; by Fusatane (Isshōsai), Hiroshige (Ichiryūsai), Kunichika, Kunihisa, Kunisada (Toyokuni 2nd, Gototei), Kunisada 2nd (Baichōrō), Kuniteru (Ichiyūsai), Kuniyoshi (Ichiyūsai), Toyokuni, Yoshichika (Ikkeisai), and Yoshitsuya (Ichiyeisai). *100 sheets.* (13½ × 9½).
O1. D. 3.

————— Portraits of Women, and Amusements of the Seasons; by Fusatane, Hiroshige, Kunichika, Kunimaro (Ichiyensai), Kunisada (Toyokuni 2nd, Kachōrō, Ichiyōsai), Kunisada 2nd (Baichōrō), Kuniteru (Ichiyūsai), Kuniyoshi (Ichiyūsai), Sadahide (Gyokuran), Toyokuni, and Yoshichika (Ikkeisai). *100 sheets.* (13¼ × 9½).
O1. D. 4.

————— Theatrical and Legendary Scenes; by Hokuchō (Shunshosai), Hokushū (Shunkōsai), Hokuyei (Shunkōsai), Kunisada (Toyokuni 2nd, Kachōrō, Gototei), Kuniyoshi (Ichiyūsai), Shigeharu (Gyokuryūtei, Ryūsai), Toyokuni, Yeizan, Yoshikuni (Shumkōdō), and Yoshitora. *60 sheets.* (14¼ × 9¾).
O1. D. 5.

ALBUM.—Portraits of Women, Theatrical Characters, and various popular Scenes; by Hiroshige, Keisai (Yeisen), Kunikane, Kunisada (Toyokuni 2nd, Gototei, Kachōrō, Ichiyōsai), Kunisada 2nd (Ichijusai), Kuniyasu, Kuniyoshi (Ichiyūsai, Chōōrō), Sadafusa (Gokitei), Sadahide (Gyokuransai), Sadakage (Gokotei), Toyokuni, and Yoshitora (Ichimōsai). *89 sheets.* (14½ × 10).

Ol. D. 6.

———— Portraits of Women, and Amusements of the Seasons; by Keisai (Yeisen), Kunisada (Toyokuni 2nd), Kunisada 2nd, and Toyokuni. *60 sheets.* (14¼ × 9¾).

Ol. D. 7.

———— Scenes from Theatrical Plays, the novel "Genji Monogatari," etc.; by Kuniaki, Kunisada (Toyokuni 2nd, Gototei, Kachōrō, Ki-ō), Kunisada 2nd (Baichōrō), Kunitomi (Kwasentei), Kuniyasu, Kuniyoshi (Ichiyūsai), Sadafusa (Gokitei), Sahahide (Gountei), Yoshikazu (Ichijusai), and Yoshitora. *96 sheets.* (13¾ × 9¼).

Ol. D. 8.

———— Portraits of Women, Picnic Parties, Street Scenes, etc.; by Hiroshige, Keisai (Yeisen), Kunimasa (Ichijusai), Kunimori (Ippōsai), Kunisada (Toyokuni 2nd, Ichiyōsai, Kachōrō, Gototei), Kunisada 2nd (Baichōrō), Kuniteru, Kuniyoshi (Ichiyūsai), Sadahide (Gyokurantei), Shigenobu, Toyokuni, Yoshifuji, and Yoshikazu (Ichijusai). *110 sheets.* (13¾ × 9¼).

Ol. D. 9.

———— Portraits of Women, Picnic Scenes, Travellers crossing the river Ōi, a Procession, etc.; by Hiroshige, Kunimori (Ippōsai), Kunisada (Toyokuni 2nd, Kachōrō, Gototei, Ichiyōsai, Kokuteisha), Kuniyoshi (Ichiyūsai), Sadahide (Gountei), Sadayuki, Shigenobu, Toyokuni, and Yeizan. *126 sheets.* (13¼ × 9½).

Ol. D. 10.

———— Portraits of Women, Scenes from the novel "Genji Monogatari," Traditional personages, and Landscapes; by Chikamaro, Hiroshige, Keisai (Yeisen), Kunisada 2nd (Baichōrō), Kunitsuna (Ichiransai), Kuniyoshi, Toyokuni, Yoshitoshi (Ikkwaisai), and Yoshitsuya (Ichiyeisai). *98 sheets.* (13 × 9).

Ol. D. 11.

TOYOKUNI.—Scenes from the novel "Genji Monogatari." *45 sheets.* (14¼ × 10).

Ol. D. 2.

ALBUM.—Azuma Nishikiye. Coloured pictures of Yedo, the Eastern Capital, Pictures of Genji Court Amusements, Picnics, and celebrated Personages ; by Hiroshige, Kuniaki, Kunimaro, Kunimaru, Kunimasa, Kunisada (Toyokuni 2nd, Kachōrō, Ichiyōsai, Kokuteisha), Kunisada 2nd (Baichōrō), **Kuniteru** (Ichiyūsai), Kuniyoshi (Ichiyūsai, Chōōrō), **Sadafusa**, Sadahide, Sadahiko, Sadahiro, Sadakage, Sadamasu, Sadamura, Sadashige, Sadatoshi, Toyokuni, Yoshifuji, **Yoshifusa**, **Yoshihisa**, **Yoshiju**, Yoshikatsu, Yoshikono, Yoshimaru, Yoshimasa, **Yoshinori**, Yoshitada, Yoshitoyo, **Yoshitsuna**, and Yoshitsuya. *244 sheets.* (14½ × 10). **Ol. E. 1.**

This book was the property of Mori Takamune of Ōsaka, and was bound by Watanabe. At the end is an inscription by the owner, " I had " great trouble to collect all of these, but at last succeeded in com- " pleting it in the 3rd year of Bunkyu (1863)."

—————— Pictures of famous and beautiful **Women** in fancy dress, **Processions**, and a View of the Sumida river; by Hokushū (Shunkōsai), Keisai (Yeisen), Kunichika, Kunisada (Toyokuni 2nd, Gototei, Kachōrō), Kuniyasu, Kuniyoshi (Chōōrō, Ichiyūsai), Sadatora (Gofūtei), Shigenobu (Yanagawa), Shunkō, Shun-yō (Kintarō), Toyokuni, Yeizan, Yoshikazu (Ichijusai), Yoshikuni, and Yoshikuni (Jukōdō). *98 sheets.* (15 × 10½).

Ol. E. 2.

—————— Portraits of Actors and Women, **Amusements** of the Seasons, etc.; by Hiroshige, Hokuyei (Shumbaitei), Keisai (Yeisen), Kunichika, Kunisada (Toyokuni 2nd, Kachōrō, Ichiyōsai, Gototei), Kuniteru (Ichiyūsai), Kuniyoshi (Chōōrō), Sadahiro (Gorakutei),Sadayoshi (Kwaishuntei), Toyokuni, Yeizan, and Yoshiume (Ichiōsai). *58 sheets.* (14 × 10). **Ol. E. 3.**

—————— Pictures of **Women** engaged in various occupations, Actors off the Stage, Fishing Scenes, etc.; by Keisai (Yeisen), Kunimaru (Chōkarō), Kunisada (Toyokuni 2nd, Kachōrō), Kuniyasu, Kuniyoshi (Ichiyūsai), Sadahide (Gountei), Toyokuni, and Yeizan. *46 sheets.* (15 × 10½).

Ol. E. 5.

—————— Theatrical Scenes ; by Fusatane, Kunisada (Toyokuni 2nd, Gototei), Kunisada 2nd, Kuniyasu, Kuniyoshi (Ichiyūsai), Toyokuni, Yoshichika, and Yoshikuni. *42 sheets.* (14 × 10). **Ol. E. 6.**

ALBUM.—Theatrical Scenes, Portraits of Women, etc.; by Ashiyuki (Kegwadō), Hirosada, Hokushū (Shunkōsai), Ichigyokusai, Kunihiro, Kunihisa, Kunisada (Toyokuni 2nd, Kachōrō), Kunisada 2nd (Baichōrō), Shigeharu (Gyokuryūtei), and Yoshikuni (Jukōdō). *30 sheets.* (14¼ × 10). **O1. E. 7.**

———— Portraits of Women, and Theatrical Characters; by Keisai (Yeisen), Kunisada (Gototei), Kunisada 2nd (Baichōrō), Kuniyasu, Kuniyoshi (Chōōrō), Sadahide (Gountei), Sadatsuna (Gohōtei), Senchō (Teisai), Toyokuni (Ichiyōsai), and Yoshitora (Ichimōsai). *78 sheets.* (13½ × 9½). **O1. E. 8.**

———— Portraits of Women and Warriors, and Scenes from the drama "Chūshingura" (The Forty-seven Rōnin); by Hiroshige, Kunisada 2nd (Baichōrō), Kuniyoshi (Ichiyūsai), Yoshitaki (Ichiyōtei), and Yoshiume. *28 sheets.* (10 × 7). **O5. A. 8.**

———— Theatrical Characters, Portraits of Warriors, Wrestlers, etc.; by Hirosada, Hokuyei (Shumbaisai), Kunichika, Kunisada (Toyokuni 2nd, Kachōrō), Kuniteru (Ichiyōsai), Kuniyoshi (Ichiyūsai), Sadamasu (Gochōtei), and Toyokuni. *38 sheets.* (14 × 10). **O5. A. 9.**

SECTION VII*a*.—MILITARY COSTUME

(INCLUDING ARMS AND ARMOUR).

AKATSUKI Kanenari.—Ningyō Zuye. Pictures of popular Heroes, forming subjects for Ornaments in the festival of the Shintō Temple Temmangū, in Ōsaka; compiled by Akatsuki Kanenari, illustrated by Matsugawa Hanzan. *Cuts.* (9 × 7), 1846. **O3. C. 4.**

ARMOUR.—Shūko Jisshu. Armour, Helmets, Weapons, etc. *Cuts.* 12 vols. (15 × 10). **O4. B. 4.**

CHILDREN.—Yehon Yamato Warambe. Pictures of Children at Play, Warriors, etc. *Cuts.* 3 vols. in 2 (9 × 6). **O5. D. 36.**

HISTORY.—Yehon Sangokushi. History of the War between the Three Dynasties, Shoku, Gi, and Go. *Cuts.* Vols. 3, 4, 6, of a set. (9 × 6). **O5. D. 47.**

HOKUSAI.—Yehon Musashi Abumi. Pictures of famous Warriors; by Hokusai (at the age of 77), engraved by Yegawa Tomekichi. *Cuts*. Vol. 2. (9 × 6) Yedo, 1836. **O5. E. 34.**

————Yehon Suikoden. The Hundred and Eight Heroes and Heroines from the Chinese novel "Suikoden." *Cuts*. (9 × 6), 1829. **O3. E. 21.**

————Kwachō Sansui Saigwa Zushiki. Designs for Art Metal-work. *Cuts*. Vols. 3, 4, of a set of 5. (5 × 7) Yedo, 1863–64. **O4. D. 2.**

INSCRIPTIONS.—Shūko Jisshu—Heiki (Weapons). Inscriptions on Banners. *Cuts*. 5 vols. (15 × 10). **O4. A. 6.**

KEISAI, Yeisen.—Buyū Sakigake Zuye. Portraits of Heroes and Heroines. *Cuts*. Vols. 1, 2, of a series. (9 × 6) Nagoya, Owari. **O5. E. 35.**

———— Yeiyū Gwashi. Portraits of Heroes and Heroines. *Cuts*. (9 × 6), 1836. **O5. D. 6.**

KŌSUISAI, Kitao.—Yehon Yaso Ujikawa. Famous Japanese and Chinese Heroes, with verses of humorous poetry; illustrated by Kitao Kōsuisai. *Cuts*. 3 vols. in 1. (9 × 6), 1786. **O5. D. 11.**

KUNIYOSHI, Ichiyūsai, and YOSHIKAZU, Ichijusai.—Portraits of famous historical Personages, with verses of poetry. *Cuts, col.* (14½ × 9¾). **O4. G. 14.**

ROBUN, Kanagaki.—Shōzō Suiko Meimeiden. Short sketches of the Hundred and Eight Heroes and Heroines from the Chinese novel "Suikoden"; by Kanagaki Robun. Illustrated by Ichiunsai Kunihisa, and Kunifusa. *Cuts*. 4 vols. (7 × 5), 1856. **O4. C. 23.**

TAKEKIYO, Kaan.—Yehon Kunkō-shō. Short stories of noted Personages; illustrated by Kaan Takekiyo. *Cuts, col.* Vols. 1, 2, of a set of 10. (9 × 6) Yedo, 1838. **O5. E. 36.**

WEAPONS.—Shūko Jisshu—Heiki (Weapons). Bows, Arrows, Quivers, etc. *Cuts*. 2 vols. (15 × 10). **O4. B. 5.**

———— Shūko Jisshu—Heiki (Weapons). Swords, Daggers, and Fittings of Weapons. *Cuts*. 3 vols. (15 × 10). **O4. B. 6.**

KU-KWA.- Koku-Kwa (National Flower). A selection
of the best examples of Japanese Fine Art,with
explanatory Notes by various authors,repros. of
famous Pictures & ill. of typical specimens of
Industrial Art. Ed. by Rokusaburo Yamamoto,& others.
Plates,some col. & ill. in the text. (16x11)
Tōkyō, 1889. also an ed. with some English text.
02.E.1.

ΒΟΤΑ Beisen,& Beisai.-Nisshin Sentō Gwahō. Ill.
account of the Japanese-Chinese War. cuts,col.
vols. 1-5,8,of a set.(7x9) Tōkyō,1894-95.
04.D.14.

See 05.E.40. page.57

YEGUCHI Shusai.- Keiki "Karabein" susei. Manual of
Musketry & Horsemanship for Cavalry. Trans. from
the Dutch by Yeguchi Shusai. Ed. by Sawaki Yoshi-
inosuke. cuts,col. Vol.1 of (?) 2. (10x7) Matsuma
Ansei 3 (A.D. 1856).   08.B.11.
    "Karabein" is derived from the Duthch word
    cavalry.

Yōsai, Kikuchi.—Zenken Kojitsu. Characters in Japanese
History. *Cuts.* Vols. 1 (part 2), 3 (part 1), 4, 5 (part 1),
8, 9, of a set of about 20 vols., each in two parts. (10 × 7)

05. F. 8.

* Vols 1 & 2 (each incomplete) 05.E.36
  Note :— 05.E.40 is a reprint.

YAMAMOTO Rokusaburo.—Koku-kwa (National Flower).
A selection of the best examples of Japanese Fine Art,
with explanatory Notes by various authors, repro- *see*
ductions of famous Pictures, and illustrations of typical *Kof-uwa.*
specimens of Industrial Art. Edited by Rokusaburo
Yamamoto. *Plates, some col., and illustrations in the*
text. (16 × 11) Tōkyō, 1889– O2. E. 1.

✳ YAMAZAKI Tomo-o.—Yehon Kunkō-gusa. Short Sketches
of the Lives of distinguished Personages. Illustrated in
colour by Kaan Takekiyo. *Cuts, col.* 5 vols. (9 × 6)
Yedo, 1839– O5. E. 40.

YOSHIKAZU, Ichijusai. —Pictures of Warriors by Ichijusai
Yoshikazu ; and Comical Pictures of the great earth-
quake in 1855, by unknown artists. *Cuts, col.* (10 × 7).
O5. C. 18.

ALBUMS OF PRINTS IN COLOUR.

ALBUM.—Battle, and other Scenes, Military Processions,
etc. ; by Kunimasa (Ichiyūsai), Kunisada (Toyokuni 2nd,
Gototei), Kuniteru (Ichiyōsai), Kuniyasu, Kuniyoshi
(Ichiyūsai), Sadahide (Gyokuransai), Sadatora (Gofūtei),
Shuntei, Toyokuni (Ichiyōsai), Yoshiharu (Ichibaisai),
Yoshikado (Ichirinsai), Yoshikazu (Ichijusai), Yoshimune
(Isshōsai), Yoshitora (Ichimōsai), Yoshitsuru (Isseisai),
and Yoshitsuya (Ichiyeisai). *107 sheets.* (14½ × 10).
O1. A. 25.

——— Battle and Theatrical Scenes, Portraits of Warriors,
etc. ; by Hokui, Kunisada (Toyokuni 2nd), Kuniyoshi,
Ryūsai, Sadahide, Sadashige, Tominobu, Toyokuni,
Yoshifuji, Yoshikazu, Yoshitora, and Yoshitsuya. *62*
sheets. (13¾ × 9¾). O1. A. 26.

——— Portraits of Heroes, Theatrical Scenes, etc. ; by
Ichiryūsai, Kunisada (Toyokuni 2nd), Kuniyoshi, Nao-
masa, and Toyokuni. *67 sheets.* (14 × 10). O1. A. 27.

——— Battle Scenes, Caricatures, etc. ; by Kunitsuna,
Kuniyoshi (Ichiyūsai), Ōsai, Sadahide (Gountei), Toyo-
kuni, Yoshichika (Ikkeisai), Yoshifusa (Ippōsai), Yoshi-
mori, Yoshitora (Ichimōsai), Yoshitoshi (Ikkwaisai), and
Yoshitsuna (Ittōsai). *51 sheets.* (14 × 10).
O1. A. 28.

ALBUM.—Battle Scenes, and a Bird's Eye View of the noted places in the Western Provinces ; by Hideteru, Kunichika, Kunihisa, Kunimitsu, Kuniteru, Sadahide, Yoshikazu, Yoshitora, and Yoshitoshi. *41 sheets.* (14½ × 9¾).

Ol. A. 29.

———— Amusements of the Seasons, Pictures of Women and Warriors, etc. ; by Kunimaro (Ichiyensai), Kuniteru (Ichiyūsai), Kuniyoshi (Ichiyūsai), Toyokuni, and Yoshifuji (Ippōsai). *102 sheets.* (14½ × 10½) **Ol. B. 18.**

———— Portraits of Women, and Historical Scenes (including a set of Portraits of Mikado); by Chikanobu (Yōshūsai), Hiroshige, Kunichika (Toyohara), Kunihisa (Ichiryūsai), Kunihisa (Ippōsai), Kunisada (Toyokuni 2nd), Kunisada 2nd, Kuniyoshi (Ichiyūsai), Sadanobu (Hasegawa), Senchō (Sogetsuyen), Toyokuni, and Yoshitoshi (Oso). *38 sheets.* (14¼ × 10). **Ol. B. 19.**

———— Portraits of Women and Warriors, Theatrical, Battle, and other Scenes, etc. ; by Hiroshige, Kunisada (Toyokuni 2nd), Kuniyasu, Toyohiro, and Toyokuni. *89 sheets.* (14½ × 10). **Ol. B. 20.**

———— Historical and Traditional Scenes ; by Hiroshige, Kunisada (Toyokuni 2nd), Kuniyoshi, Yoshifuji, Yoshikatsu, Yoshitora, and Yoshitsuru. *71 sheets.* (14½ × 10). **Ol. B. 21.**

———— Scenes in the Lives of Yoritomo, and Yoshitsune ; by Kunikiyo (Utagawa), Kunisada 2nd (Baichōrō), Sadahide (Gountei), and Yoshitora. *12 sheets.* (14½ × 9¾). **Ol. B. 22.**

———— Battle, Historical, Traditional, and Theatrical Scenes, etc. ; by Kuniyoshi, Sadahide, Yoshikazu, Yoshitora, and Yoshitsuya. *70 sheets.* (14½ × 10). **Ol. B. 23.**

———— Pictures of famous Heroes, Historical and other Scenes, Humorous sketches, etc. ; by Kunisada (Toyokuni 2nd), Kuniyoshi, Sadahide (Gountei), Yoshichika (Ikkeisai), Yoshiharu (Ichibaisai), Yoshikazu (Ichijusai), and Yoshitoshi (Ikkwaisai). *62 sheets.* (14¼ × 10). **Ol. B. 24.**

———— Portraits of Women, Theatrical Characters and Warriors ; by Keisai (Yeisen), Kunisada (Toyokuni 2nd), Kuniyasu, Kuniyoshi, and Toyokuni. *26 sheets.* (14½ × 10¼). **O2. B. 33.**

SANBA,Shikitei.- Yedzu Yakusha Sangaikyo. Three
   Stories of the pleasant Theatre. Ill by Utagawa
   Toyokuni (1) Cuts,col. 2 vols. (9x6) Yedo,
   Kwansei 13, 1st.month (A.D.1800)   08.8.18.
   Lit. "three-storied recreation," a punning
   allusion to the three storied theatrical buildin
   & the three realms of Existence of the Buddhists
   viz. Past,Present,Future. publishers, Yorodzuya
   Nishinomiya.

* The last page is signed Utagawa Kunisada
   & dated Tempo 14 = 1843 but neither appears to
   refer to present volume.

ALBUM.—Landscapes, and Illustrations of Warriors; by Hiroshige, Keisai (Yeisen), and Kuniyoshi. *13 sheets.* (10 × 14). **O4. F. 4.**

SECTION VII*b.*—THEATRICAL COSTUME

(INCLUDING THAT OF PROFESSIONAL BEAUTIES, SINGING GIRLS, ETC.).

COSTUME.—Theatrical Characters. *Cuts.* (11 × 7). **O3. F. 11.**

DRAMA.—Yehon Datekurabe Kashiku-no Benigasa. A Drama. *Cuts.* 5 vols. (9 × 6). **O5. E. 37.**

FUSATANE Isshōsai, KUNIKIYO, and TOYOKUNI Ichiyōsai.— Scenes from the Drama "Chūshingura" (the Story of the Forty-seven Rōnin). A set of 12 by each artist. *Cuts, col.* (8¾ × 13). **O4. F. 5.**

HOKUSAI.—Yehon Wakan-no Homare. Noted Japanese and Chinese Heroes; by Hokusai (at the age of 76). *Cuts, tinted.* (9 × 6), 1850. **O3. E. 22.**

Another copy. *Cuts.* (9 × 6), 1850. **O3. E. 23.**

MORIKUNI, Kōsoken Tachibana.—Yehon Ōshukubai. Pictures of noted Personages, Birds and Flowers; Drawing Lessons in styles of various artists, etc. *Cuts.* Vols. 2-7 of a set of 7. (9 × 6) Naniwa (Ōsaka), 1740. **O3. D. 2.**

NŌ DANCE.—Pictures of Nō Dancers. *Cuts, col.* (7 × 2). **O4. C. 25.**

SHŌKŌSAI Hambei. — Gakuya Zuye, Shūi. Illustrated description of a Stage Play; with the scenes behind the Stage, construction of Puppets, theatrical Portraits, etc.; illustrated by Shōkōsai Hambei. Supplement to "Gakuya Zuye." *Cuts, some col.* Vol. 2 of a set of 2. (10 × 7). **O3. F. 12.**

✳ THEATRES—Gekijō Ikkwan Mushimegane. Remarks on Theatrical Stages, Plays, etc. *Cuts, col.* The last vol. of a set. (9 × 6), 1831. **O5. E. 38.**

THEATRICAL SCENES.—Theatrical Scenes. *Cuts.* (9 × 6). **O5. E. 39.**

Tokushō, Goryūtei.—Kowairo Hayagaten. Collection of extracts from several Dramas with Portraits of the Actors; for the use of beginners. Illustrated by Kachōrō Kunisada. *Cuts.* Vol. 1 of a series. (7 × 5), 1831. **O4. C. 24.**

Toyokuni.—Kunizukushi Yamato-no Homare. Theatrical Characters with a reference to each province of Japan; the supplementary pictures by pupils of Toyokuni. *Cuts, col., and mounted.* (9¾ × 7). **O5. C. 19.**

ALBUMS OF PRINTS IN COLOUR.

ALBUM.—Theatrical Characters, Portraits of Women, etc., and various Scenes; by Hiroshige, Kunisada (Toyokuni 2nd, Gototei), Kuniyoshi (Ichiyūsai), Sadahide (Gofūtei), Shigeharu (Ryūsai), Toyokuni, and Yoshitsuya (Ichiyeisai). *66 sheets.* (14 × 9¾). **O1. A. 30.**

———— Theatrical Scenes, Building the Castle of Chihaya, etc.; by Hiroshige, Kuniyoshi, Toyokuni, Yoshifuji, and Yoshimori. *47 sheets,* (14½ × 10). **O1. A. 31.**

———— Portraits of Women, Theatrical Characters, and Legendary Scenes; by Fusatane, Hiroshige, Hokuyei (Shumbaisai), Hokuyei (Shunkōsai), Keisai (Yeisen), Kunichika, Kunimasa (Ichijusai), Kunisada (Toyokuni 2nd, Gototei, Kachōrō, Ichiyōsai), Kunisada 2nd, Kuniteru (Ichiyūsai), Kuniyasu, Kuniyoshi (Ichiyūsai), Shundō, Shunshō, Shunshō (Kochōyen), Shuntei, Toyokuni (Gosotei), Yoshiharu (Chōkarō), and Yoshitora (Kinchōrō). *100 sheets.* (14 × 10). **O1. A. 32.**

———— Theatrical Scenes and Characters; by Kuniyoshi, and Toyokuni. *100 sheets.* (14½ × 9¾). **O1. A. 33.**

———— Theatrical Characters; by Kunisada 2nd (Ichijusai) Kuniyoshi (Ichiyūsai), and Toyokuni. *53 sheets.* (14¼ × 10). **O1. A. 34.**

———— Scenes from the dramas "Chūshingura," "Kabuto Gunki," etc.; by Kunisada (Toyokuni 2nd), Kuniyoshi, and Toyokuni. *56 sheets.* (14½ × 10). **O1. A 35.**

———— Theatrical Scenes with Female Characters from the drama "Chūshingura"; by Kunisada (Toyokuni 2nd), Kuniyoshi, and Sadafusa. *47 sheets.* (14½ × 10). **O1. A. 36.**

SHŌ (pseud. for Ichiba Koheiji).- Yehon Yakushe
Natsu-no-Fuji. Ill. of theatrical scenes compared
with Mt.Fuji in Summer. Ill. by Katskawa Shunshō;
engr. by Mori Kichigorō. cuts. (9x6) Yedo,n.d.
(late 18th.C.)   08.8.17.
    The author considers that   theatrical repres-
entations of vice as well as of virtue have a moral
value for spectators; much as some people prefer th
bare aspect of Mt.Fuji in Summer to its Winter
appearance when covered with snow. Hence the
title. Pub.Okumura & Matsumura.

Broken Up.

Broken Up.

Broken Up.

Broken Up.

Broken Up

Broken Up,

Broken Up

Broken Up

Shunshō II (of Tōkyō)

Broken Up

Broken Up

Broken Up

Broken Up

Broken Up.

Broken Up

ALBUM.—Theatrical and other Scenes; by Hiroshige, Kunisada (Toyokuni 2nd), Kunisada 2nd, Kuniyoshi, Toyokuni, and Yoshitsuna (Ittōsai). *40 sheets.* (14¼ × 10).

Ol. A. 37.

———— Theatrical Scenes; by Kuniaki, Kunichika, Kunisada 2nd, Kunisato, Toyokuni, Yoshichika, and Yoshitsuya. *97 sheets.* (14½ × 10).

Ol. A. 38.

———— Theatrical Scenes and Characters, Processions, etc.; by Hiroshige, Kunichika, Kunisada (Toyokuni 2nd), Kunisada 2nd, Sadahide, Toyokuni, Yoshichika, and Yoshimori. *87 sheets.* (14½ × 10).

Ol. A. 39.

———— Theatrical Characters, Portraits of Women, Wrestlers, etc.; by Kunichika, Kunikazu, Kunisada (Toyokuni 2nd), Kunisada 2nd (Baichōrō), Sadafusa (Gokitei), Shunshō, Toyokuni, and Yoshichika (Ikkeisai). *33 sheets.* (14½ × 10½).

Ol. A. 40.

———— Theatrical and other Scenes, the Seven Gods of Good Fortune, Portraits, etc.; by Kunisada (Toyokuni 2nd), Kunisada 2nd, Kuniyoshi, Sadafusa, Sadahide, Sadashige, Yoshimasa, Yoshitora, and Yoshitsuya. *55 sheets.* (14¼ × 10).

Ol. A. 41.

———— Theatrical Characters, Portraits of Women, etc.; by Hiroshige, Hokusei, Keisai (Yeisen), Kunimaru (Ichiyensai), Kunisada (Toyokuni 2nd), Kunisada 2nd (Baichōrō), Kuniteru (Ichiyūsai), Kuniyoshi (Ichiyūsai), and Toyokuni. *42 sheets.* (13¾ × 10).

Ol. A. 42.

———— Portraits of Women; by Keisai (Yeisen), Kunikane, Kuniyasu, Kuniyoshi (Ichiyūsai), Sadafusā (Kitchōrō), Senchō (Teisai), Toyokuni, and Yeizan. *34 sheets.* (13¾ × 10).

Ol. A. 43.

———— Theatrical Scenes, etc.; by Kunisada (Toyokuni 2nd), Toyokuni, and Yoshitoshi. *24 sheets.* (14¼ × 10).

Ol. A. 44.

———— Theatrical Scenes, Portraits of Famous Beauties, and Warriors from the "Soga Monogatari"; by Kunihisa, Kunimasa, Kuniyoshi, and Toyokuni. *40 sheets.* (14½ × 10½).

Ol. A. 45.

———— Theatrical Scenes; by Kuniyoshi, and Toyokuni. *42 sheets.* (14½ × 10½).

Ol. A. 46.

———— Scenes from the dramas "Kagami-yama," "Kabuto-gunki," "Chūshingura," etc.; by Kunimaro, Kunisada (Toyokuni 2nd), Kuniyoshi, Sadafusa (Kitchōrō), and Yoshifuji (Ippōsai). *126 sheets.* (14 × 10¼). **Ol. A. 47.**

ALBUM.—Theatrical Scenes; by Kunichika, Kunisada (Toyokuni 2nd), Kuniyoshi, Toyokuni, and Yoshitoshi. *100 sheets.* (14 × 10). **Ol. A. 48.**

—————— Theatrical Characters, Festival of Temma Ōsaka, etc.; by Hirosada, Hokushū (Shunkōsai), Hokuyei, Kiyoharu (Hishikawa), Sadahiro, Sadamasu (Gochōtei), Sadanobu (Hasegawa), Shigeharu (Ryūsai), and Toyohide (Kitagawa, Ichiryūtei). *49 sheets.* (14¼ × 9¾). **Ol. A. 49.**

—————— Theatrical Characters; by Kunisada (Toyokuni 2nd, Kachōrō, Ichiyōsai), and Kuniyoshi (Ichiyūsai). *46 sheets.* (14¼ × 10¼). **Ol. A. 50.**

TOYOKUNI. Album of Theatrical Scenes and Characters. *64 sheets.* (14½ × 10½). **Ol. A. 51.**

ALBUM.—Theatrical Characters; by Kunisada (Toyokuni 2nd, Gototei), and Kuniyoshi (Ichiyūsai). *77 sheets.* (14½ × 10). **Ol. B. 25.**

—————— Portraits of Women ; by Hiroshige, Keisai (Yeisen), Kiyomine, Kunisada (Toyokuni 2nd, Kachōrō, Ichiyōsai, Gototei), Kunisada 2nd (Baichōrō), Kuniyoshi (Ichiyūsai), Shunchō, Toyokuni, Yeizan, and Yoshitora (Kinchōrō). *34 sheets.* (14½ × 9½). **Ol. B. 26.**

—————— Portraits of Women ; by Keisai (Yeisen), Kunisada (Toyokuni 2nd, Gototei, Kachōrō), Kuniyasu (Ippōsai), Kuniyoshi (Ichiyūsai), Sadafusa (Gokitei), Sadahide (Gountei), Senchō (Sogetsuyen), Toyokuni, Yeizan, Yoshichika (Ikkeisai), Yoshikazu (Ichijusai), and Yoshitora (Ichimōsai). *50 sheets.* (14¾ × 9¾). **Ol. B. 27.**

—————— Portraits of Women, Theatrical Characters, Amusements of the Seasons, etc. ; by Hiroshige, Keisai (Yeisen), Kunisada (Toyokuni 2nd), Kunisada 2nd (Baichōrō), Kuniteru (Ichiyūsai), Kunitsuna (Ichiransai), Kuniyoshi (Ichiyūsai), Toyokuni, and Yoshichika. *72 sheets.* (14½ × 9¾). **Ol. B. 28.**

—————— Portraits of Women, Theatrical Scenes, Amusements of the Seasons, etc. ; by Keisai (Yeisen), Kunisada (Toyokuni 2nd, Kachōrō), Kunisada 2nd (Baichōrō), Kunisato (Ryūsensai), Kuniteru, Kuniyoshi, Senchō (Sogetsuyen), Tominobu (Kwasentei), Toyokuni, Yeizan, and Yoshitora. *68 sheets.* (14½ × 9¾). **Ol. B. 29.**

Broken Up.

Broken Up

Broken Up.

Broken Up.

Broken Up.

Broken Up.

Broken Up.

Broken Up

Broken Up.

Broken Up

Broken Up.

Broken Up.

Broken Up.

Broken Up.

Broken Up.

Broken Up

Broken Up

ALBUM.—Theatrical Scenes, Portraits of Women, etc.; by
Ashiyuki (Kegwadō), Hidekuni (Toyokawa), Hokuchō
(Shunshōsai), Hokushū (Shunkōsai), Keisai (Yeisen),
Kunisada (Toyokuni 2nd, Gototei), Kuniyasu, Sadafusa
(Gokitei), Shibakuni (Saikwōtei), Shunshi (Seiyōsai),
Toyokuni, Umekuni (Toyokawa), and Yoshikuni (Toyo-
kawa). *62 sheets.* (15 × 10). **O1. B. 30.**

—— Portraits of Women and Famous Characters in
various Scenes; by Hiroshige, Kunisada (Toyokuni 2nd),
Kuniyoshi, and Toyokuni. *28 sheets.* (14½ × 10½).
O1. B. 31.

—— Portraits of Women; by Keisai (Yeisen), Kunisada (Toyokuni 2nd, Gototei), Kuniyasu (Ippōsai), Sadatora (Gofūtei), Toyokuni, and Yeizan. *44 sheets.*
(14¾ × 10½). **O1. B. 32.**

—— Portraits of Women, etc.; by Hiroshige, Kunisada
(Toyokuni 2nd), Kuniyoshi, and Toyokuni. *60 sheets.*
(14¾ × 10). **O1. B. 33.**

—— Theatrical and Historical Characters, Scenes from
the Life of Ōishi Yoshi-ō, the Chief of the Forty-seven
Rōnin, etc.; by Ashiyuki (Kegwadō), Hirosada, Hiroshige, Hokumyō (Shunkōsai), Kunisada (Toyokuni 2nd),
and Kuniyoshi (Ichiyūsai). *40 sheets.* (14½ × 10).
O1. B. 34.

—— Theatrical Portraits and Scenes; by Kunimori,
Kunisada (Toyokuni 2nd), Kuniyoshi, and Toyokuni.
14 sheets. (9¾ × 14½). **O1. B. 35.**

—— Theatrical Scenes, etc.; by Kunimaru (Ichiyensai),
Kunisada (Toyokuni 2nd), Reizan, Shinshi, and Toyokuni. *41 sheets.* (15 × 10½). **O1. B. 36.**

—— Theatrical Characters; by Kunihiro, Kunisada
(Toyokuni 2nd, Gototei), Nagakuni, Shunkō, and Toyokuni. *16 sheets.* (14½ × 10½). **O1. B. 37.**

—— Theatrical Scenes, and Portraits of Women; by
Kunisada (Toyokuni 2nd, Gototei, Kachōrō), and Kuniyoshi (Ichiyūsai). *34 sheets.* (14¾ × 10½). **O1. B. 38.**

—— Scenes from the drama "Chūshingura," etc.; by
Kunisada (Toyokuni 2nd), and Kuniyoshi. *10 sheets.*
(15 × 10½). **O1. B. 39.**

ALBUM.—Portraits of Women, and Theatrical Characters; by Keisai (Yeisen), Kunisada (Toyokuni 2nd, Gototei, Kachōrō), Kuniyoshi (Ichiyūsai), **Sadatora** (Gofūtei), and Toyokuni. *56 sheets.* (14¾ × 10).   **O1. B. 40.**

———— Scenes from the drama "Taikōki," etc.; by Kunisada (Toyokuni 2nd, Gototei), and Kuniyoshi (Ichiyūsai). *23 sheets.* (14½ × 10).   **O1. B. 41.**

———— Portraits of Women, and Theatrical Characters; by Keisai (Yeisen), Kunisada (Toyokuni 2nd, Gototei), and Kuniyasu. *23 sheets.* (15 × 10¾).   **O1. B. 42.**

———— Theatrical Scenes, Pictures of Nobles and Ladies, Portraits of Women, etc.; by Hiroshige, Kunichika (Ichiōsai), Kunisada (Toyokuni 2nd, Kachōrō, Ichiyōsai, Gototei), Kunisada 2nd (Baichōrō), Kunisato, Kuniyoshi (Chōōrō, Ichiyūsai), ~~Shōjōsai~~, Toyokuni, Yoshikazu (Ichijusai), and Yoshitora. *91 sheets.* (14½ × 10).   **O2. C. 1.**

KUNIYOSHI, Chōōrō, Ichiyūsai. — Theatrical Characters, each with a Poem, from the novel "Genji Monogatari." *54 sheets.* (14 × 9¼).   **O1. C. 14.**

ALBUM.—Portraits of Women, and Court Nobles playing at Football; by Keisai (Yeisen), and Kunisada (Toyokuni 2nd, Kachōrō). *40 sheets.* (15 × 10¼).   **O1. C. 15.**

———— Portraits of Women, Theatrical Scenes, Views of Noted Places in Yedo, etc.; by Hiroshige, Keisai (Yeisen), Kunisada (Toyokuni 2nd), **Kunisada 2nd**, Toyokuni, Utamaro, Yeizan, Yoshichika, and Yoshishige. *30 sheets.* (14½ × 9½).   **O1. C. 16.**

————Theatrical Characters, Portraits of Women, Travellers crossing the river Ōi, etc.; by Ashiyuki (Kegwadō), Harusada (Gwachōken), Hokuchō (Shunshōsai), Hokumyō (Sekkōtei), Hokuyei (Shumbaisai), Kunichika (Ikkeisai), Kunihiro, Kunimasa (Ichijusai), Kunisada 2nd (Baichōrō), Kuniyoshi (Ichiyūsai), Shigeharu (Gyokuryūtei, Ryūsai), Shunkō, Toyokuni, Yoshichika (Ikkeisai), Yoshikuni (Jukōdō), and Yoshitora (Kinchōrō). *32 sheets.* (14½ × 10½).   **O1. C. 17.**

Broken Up.

Broken Up.

Broken Up.

Kiōsai (Shōjō).

broken Up.

A duplicate copy of this is kept as an example of Binding being bound in grass cloth - (undressed).

Broken Up

Broken Up

Broken Up.

65

ALBUM.—Theatrical Characters, View of Asakusa, and the Interior of a Theatre; by Hiroshige, Hokuyei (Shunkōsai), Kunihiro, Kunisada (Toyokuni 2nd, Gototei, Kachōrō), Kuniyoshi (Ichiyūsai), Sadatora (Gofūtei), and Shigeharu (Gyokuryūtei). *56 sheets.* (14½ × 10).
Ol. C. 18.

———— Portraits of Women, Theatrical Characters, etc.; by Keisai (Yeisen), Kiyomine, Kunihiro, Kunisada (Toyokuni 2nd), Kuniyasu, Kuniyoshi, Shigenobu, Toyokuni,Yeizan, Yoshikuni (Jukōdō), and Yūrakusai. *44 sheets.* (14½ × 9½).
Ol. C. 19.

———— TheatricalScenes; by Ashiyuki (Kegwadō), Hokumyō (Shunkōsai), Hokuyei (Shunkōsai), Kunihiro, Kunisada (Toyokuni 2nd, Gototei), Kuniyoshi (Ichiyūsai), Sadatora (Gofūtei). Senchō (Teisai), Shigeharu, and Toyokuni. *91 sheets.* (14¾ × 10¼).
Ol. C. 20.

———— Portraits of Women, etc.; by Hiroshige, Keisai (Yeisen), Kuniaki, Kunisada (Toyokuni 2nd, Kachōrō, Ichiyōsai). Kuniyoshi (Chōōrō, Ichiyūsai), Shunkō, Shunshō (Hōrai), Tominobu (Kwasentei), Toyokuni, Yeizan (Kikugawa), Yoshifuji, and Yoshitora (Kinchōrō). *36 sheets.* (14½ × 10).
Ol. C. 21.

———— Portraits of Women, and Theatrical Scenes; by Keisai (Yeisen), Kiyomine, Kunisada (Toyokuni 2nd, Gototei, Kachōrō), Kuniyasu, Kuniyoshi (Ichiyūsai), Sadafusa (Gokitei), Toyokuni, and Yeizan. *38 sheets.* (14½ × 10¼).
Ol. C. 22.

———— Portraits of Women, Heroines, and Theatrical Scenes; by Ashiyuki, Hokuchō (Shunshōsai), Hokushū, Keisai (Yeisen), Kuniharu, Kunihiro, Kunimaru, Kuninao, Kunisada (Toyokuni 2nd, Gototei), Kuniyasu (Ippōsai), Kuniyoshi, Sadamasa, Shibakuni (Saikwōtei), Shunsen, Shunshi (Gwatoken), Shuntei, Toyokuni, Toyoshige (Ichiryūsai), and Yeizan. *76 sheets.* (15 × 10½).
Ol. C. 23.

———— Portraits of Women; by Keisai (Yeisen), Kuninao, Kunisada (Toyokuni 2nd, Gototei), Kuniyasu, Kuniyoshi (Ichiyūsai), Sadakage (Gokotei), Senchō (Teisai), Toyokuni, and Yeizan. *114 sheets.* (15 × 10¼). **Ol. C. 24.**

ALBUM.—Portraits of Women, Theatrical Characters, etc.; by Ashiyuki (Kegwadō), Hokuyei (Shunkōsai), Keisai (Yeisen), Kunikane, Kuninao, Kuniyasu (Ippōsai), Nobukatsu, Shigeharu (Ryūsai), and Yoshikuni (Jukōdō). *25 sheets.* (15 × 10). **Ol. C. 25.**

—— Theatrical Characters, and Portraits of Women; by Ashimaro, Hokuyei (Shunkōsai), Keisai (Yeisen), Kuniharu, Kunimaru, Kunisada (Toyokuni 2nd, Gototei), Kuniyasu, Kuniyoshi (Ichiyūsai), Toyokuni, and Yoshifuji. *20 sheets.* (14½ × 10). **Ol. C. 26.**

—— Theatrical Characters, Portraits of Women, and various Scenes; by Hiroshige, Keisai (Yeisen), Kunihiro, Kunisada (Toyokuni 2nd, Gototei, Kachōrō), Kunisada 2nd (Baichōrō), Kuniyasu, Kuniyoshi (Ichiyūsai), Sadafusa (Gokitei), and Toyokuni. *118 sheets.* (14 × 10). **Ol. C. 27.**

—— Theatrical Scenes; by Ashiyuki (Kegwadō), Kuniharu, Kunisada (Toyokuni 2nd, Gototei), Kuniyasu, and Usai. *56 sheets.* (14½ × 10). **Ol. C. 28.**

—— Theatrical Characters; by Kunihiro, Kunisada (Toyokuni 2nd, Gototei), Kunitomi (Kwasentei), Kuniyasu, Kuniyoshi (Ichiyūsai), Shigeharu (Ryūsai), and Toyokuni. *60 sheets.* (14¾ × 10¼). **Ol. C. 29.**

—— Portraits of Women, Theatrical Characters, etc.; by Keisai (Yeisen), Kunimasu, Kunisada (Toyokuni 2nd), Kuniyasu, Kuniyoshi (Ichiyūsai), Sadafusa (Gokitei), Shibakuni, Shunsen, Toyokuni (Gosotei), and Yeizan. *30 sheets.* (15 × 10¼). **Ol. C. 30.**

—— Portraits of Women in various Scenes; by Hiroshige, Keisai (Yeisen), Kunisada (Toyokuni 2nd, Kachōrō), Kunisada 2nd (Baichōrō), Kuniyoshi (Ichiyūsai), Toyokuni, and Yeizan. *34 sheets.* (14 × 9½). **Ol. C. 31.**

—— Portraits of Women, Landscapes with figures, etc.; by Hiroshige, Kunisada (Toyokuni 2nd, Kachōrō, Ichiyōsai, Kokuteisha), Kunisada 2nd (Kunimasa, Ichijusai), Kuniyoshi (Ichiyūsai), Shigenobu, Shūchō (Tamagawa), Toyokuni, and Yoshitora (Ichimōsai). *28 sheets.* (14½ × 10). **Ol. C. 32.**

Broken Up.

44. A reprint of this with several additional blocks is in 02.8.24; see p. 76.

ALBUM.—Theatrical Characters, Portraits of Women, Illustrations of the Silkworm Industry, Twelve scenes from the drama "Chūshingura," etc.; by Fusatane (Isshōsai), Hiroshige, Hokuyei (Shunkōsai), Ichimaru (Jippōsha), Keisai (Yeisen, Ippitsuan), Kiyomitsu, Kunihiro, Kunisada (Toyokuni 2nd, Ichiyōsai, Kokuteisha, Kachōrō), Kuniyasu (Ippōsai), Kuniyoshi (Chōōrō, Ichiyūsai), Nobukatsu, Sadafusa (Gokitei), Sadahiro (Gorakutei), Sadayoshi (Kwaishuntei), Shigeharu (Gyokuryūtei), Shunshō, Toyokuni, Yeishō (Shinsai), Yoshifuji (Ippōsai), and Yoshitora (Ichimōsai). *60 sheets.* (14½ × 10).

O1. C. 33.

———— Theatrical Scenes; by Kuniaki, Kunichika (Ichiōsai), Kunisada (Toyokuni 2nd, Gototei, Kachōrō, Ki-ō), Kunisada 2nd (Baichōrō), Kuniyasu, Kuniyoshi (Ichiyūsai), Sadafusa (Gokitei), Toyokuni ·(Ichiyōsai), Yoshichika (Ikkeisai), Yoshitora (Ichimōsai), and Yoshitoshi (Ikkwaisai). *98 sheets.* (14 × 9½). **O1. D. 12.**

———— Theatrical Scenes, Actors at leisure, and a View of Maiko in Harima; by Hiroshige, Kuniaki, Kunichika (Ichiōsai), Kunihisa, Kunisada (Toyokuni 2nd, Gototei, Ki-ō), Kuniyoshi (Ichiyūsai), Sadahide, Toyokuni (Ichiyōsai), Yenchō (Ikkyōsai), Yoshichika (Ikkeisai), and Yoshiharu (Ichibaisai). *100 sheets.* (13¾ × 9½).

O1. D. 13.

———— Portraits of Women, Heroines, etc.; by Hiroshige, Keisai (Yeisen), Kunihisa, Kunimasa (Ichijusai), Kunimori (Ichiryūsai), Kunisada (Toyokuni 2nd, Gototei), Kuniyoshi (Chōōrō), Sadahide (Gountei), Senchō (Teisai), Shigenobu, Shunshō (Kochōyen), Toyokuni, Yoshiharu (Ichibaisai), Yoshikazu (Ichijusai), Yoshitora (Ichimōsai), and Yoshitsuya (Ichiyeisai). *100 sheets* (14 × 9½). **O1. D. 14.**

———— Portraits of Women; by Hiroshige, Keisai (Yeisen, Ippitsuan), Kunisada (Toyokuni 2nd, Kachōrō, Ichiyōsai), Kuniyasu (Ippōsai), Kuniyoshi (Ichiyūsai), Sadahide (Gyokuran), Sadatora (Gofūtei), Toyokuni, Yeizan (Kikugawa), and Yoshikazu (Ichijusai). *74 sheets.* (14½ × 9¾). **O1. D. 15.**

ALBUM.—Portraits of Women, by Hiroshige, Kunihiko, Kuniyoshi (Ichiyūsai, Chōōrō), Sadahide (Gountei, Gyokuransai), Yoshikazu (Ichijusai), Yoshitora (Ichimōsai), and Yoshitsuya (Ichiyeisai). *59 sheets.* (13¾ × 9½).

O1. D. 16.

——— Theatrical Scenes. and Portraits of Women; by Ashiyuki (Kegwadō), **Hokushū** (Shunkōsai), **Hokuyei** (Shumbaisai), Hokuyei (Shunkōsai), Keisai (Yeisen), Kitoku, Kunichika, Kunihiro, Kunimaro, Kunimori (Ippōsai), Kunisada (Toyokuni 2nd, Gototei, Kachōrō), Kuniyasu, Kuniyoshi (Ichiyūsai), Sadafusa (Gokitei), Sadamasu (Utagawa), Shigeharu (Ryūsai), Tamikuni, Yoshifuji (Ippōsai), Yoshikuni, and Yoshitora (Kinchōrō, Ichimōsai). *100 sheets.* (14 × 9½).

O1. D. 17.

——— Portraits of Women; by Keisai (Yeisen), Kuninao, Kunisada (Toyokuni 2nd, Gototei), Kuniyasu, Ryūshi, Sadakage (Gokotei), Shunkō (Shunsen), and Yeizan (Kikugawa). *60 sheets.* (13½ × 9).

O1. D. 18.

——— Theatrical Scenes; by Ashiyuki (Kegwadō), Hokushū (Shunkōsai), Hokuyei (Shumbaisai), Kunihiro (Utagawa), Kunisada (Toyokuni 2nd, Gototei), Kuniyoshi (Ichiyūsai), Sadafusa (Gokitei), Sadanobu (Hasegawa), Shigeharu (Gyokuryūtei), Shigeharu (Ryūsai), Toyokuni, Yoshikuni (Jukōdō), and Yūrakusai. *68 sheets.* (14¾ × 10).

O1. E. 4.

——— Portraits of Women, Theatrical Characters, etc.; by Ashiyuki, Hokushū (Shunkōsai), Keisai (Yeisen), Kunihiro, Kunisada (Toyokuni 2nd, Gototei, Kachōrō, Ichiyōsai), Kunisada 2nd (Baichōrō), Kunisato (Ryūsersai), Kuniyoshi (Ichiyūsai), Sadatora (Gofūtei), Sadayoshi, Shunchō, Shunkōsai, Toyokuni, Yoshikuni (Jukōdō), and Yoshitora (Kinchōrō). *50 sheets.* (14½ × 10).

O1. E. 9.

——— Theatrical Scenes, and Children at Play; by Ashikuni, Ashiyuki (Kegwadō), Hikokuni, Hokkei (Shunyōsai), Hokushū (Shunkōsai), Kunisada (Toyokuni 2nd, Kachōrō), Kunisada 2nd (Baichōrō), Shibakuni, Shunchō, Shunshō, Shun-yō, Tamikuni (Kōgwadō), Toyokuni, and Yoshikuni (Jukōdō). *50 sheets.* (14½ × 10¼).

O1. E. 10.

Broken Up.

6. _Hokushu_. grain of wood in print[a].

36. _Shunyo_.. Stencilled ground printed.

Kunisada 2nd

ALBUM.—Theatrical Scenes, Portraits of Women, Landscapes, etc.; by Ashiyuki, Fusatane, Hikokuni, Hiroshige, Hokushū (Shunkōsai), Keisai (Yeisen), Kunihiro, Kunihisa, Kunisada (Toyokuni 2nd, Kokuteisha, Kachōrō, Ichiyōsai), Kunisada 2nd (Baichōrō), Kuniyoshi (Ichiyūsai), Shibakuni (Saikwōtei), Shigenobu, Tamikuni, Yoshichika, Yoshifuji, and Yoshikuni. *60 sheets.* (14½ × 10¼). **O1. E. 11.**

—— Theatrical Scenes, Portraits of Women, Landscapes, etc.; by Ashiyuki, Hikokuni, Hokushū (Shunkōsai), Kunihiro (Gwanjōsai), Kunisada (Toyokuni 2nd, Kokuteisha, Kachōrō), Kuniyoshi (Ichiyūsai), Shibakuni (Saikwōtei), Shunchō, Shunshō Shun-yō, Shun-yō (Kintarō), Tamikuni (Kōgwadō), Toyokuni (Ichiyōsai), and Yoshikuni. *60 sheets.* (14½ × 10¼). **O1. E. 12.**

—— Portraits of Women; by Hokuyei (Shunkōsai), Keisai (Yeisen, Ippitsuan), Kunisada (Toyokuni 2nd, Gototei, Kachōrō), Kunisada 2nd (Baichōrō), Kuniyasu (Ippōsai), Kuniyoshi (Chōōrō, Ichiyūsai), Sadatora (Gofūtei), Shunshō (Kochōrō), Toyokuni, and Yoshitora (Kinchōrō, Ichimōsai). *60 sheets.* (13½ × 9½). **O1. E. 13.**

—— Portraits of Women with Verses addressed to them; by Keisai (Yeisen), Kunisada (Toyokuni 2nd, Gototei, Kachōrō), Kuniyasu (Ippōsai), Kuniyoshi (Ichiyūsai), Sadakage (Gokotei), Senchō (Teisai), Toyokuni, and Yeizan (Kikugawa). *54 sheets.* (13½ × 9½). **O1. E. 14.**

—— Portraits of Women; by Hokuyei (Shumbaisai), Keisai (Yeisen, Ippitsuan), Kunimaro (Shōchōrō), Kunisada (Toyokuni 2nd, Kachōrō, Gototei), Kunitomi (Kwasentei), Kuniyasu, Kuniyoshi (Chōōrō, Ichiyūsai), Senchō (Teisai, Sogetsuyen), Toyokuni (Gosotei, Ichiyōsai) Yeizan (Kikugawa), and Yoshitora (Ichimōsai). *52 sheets.* (13½ × 9½). **O1. E. 15.**

—— Portraits of Women; by Hiroshige, Ichigyokusai, Keisai (Yeisen), Kunihiro, Kunisada (Toyokuni 2nd, Kokuteisha, Ichiyūsai, Gototei, Kachōrō), Kuniyoshi (Ichiyūsai), Sadafusa (Gokitei), Sadatora (Gofūtei), Toyokuni, and Yoshikazu (Ichijusai). *52 sheets.* (13½ × 9½). **O1. E. 16.**

ALBUM.—Theatrical Scenes ; by Hiroshige, Kunichika, Kunimasa, Kunisada (Toyokuni 2nd, Ichiyōsai, Kachōro, Ki-ō), Kunisato, Kuniyoshi (Ichiyūsai, Chōōrō), Sadanobu, Toyokuni, and Yoshitora (Kinchōrō, Ichimōsai). *78 sheets.* (14¼ × 9¾).   **O1. E. 17.**

———— Portraits of Women ; by Hōyen (Ichiyōsai), Kunichika, Kunisada (Toyokuni 2nd, Gototei, Kachōro, Kokuteisha), Kuniyoshi (Chōōrō, Ichiyūsai), Sadahide (Gyokurantei), Toyokuni (Gosotei, Ichiyōsai), Yoshitora (Ichimōsai, Kinchōrō), and Yoshitsuya (Ichiyeisai). *98 sheets.* (14 × 9¾).   **O1. E. 18.**

———— Portraits of famous and beautiful Women ; by Hokuyei (Sekkwaro), Kunisada (Toyokuni 2nd), Kuniyoshi (Ichiyūsai, Chōōrō), Sadahide (Gountei), Sadahiro (Gochōtei), Shigeharu (Ryūtei), Shigenobu, and Toyokuni. *36 sheets.* (14½ × 10).   **O1. E. 19.**

———— Pictures of Women in various Scenes, Theatrical Characters, the Ceremony of setting up the frame-work of a House, etc. ; by Keisai (Yeisen), Kunisada (Toyokuni 2nd, Kachōrō), Kuniyasu, Kuniyoshi (Ichiyūsai), Sadafusa (Gokitei), Sadahide, Sadakane, and Toyokuni. *150 sheets.* (14½ × 10).   **O1. E. 20.**

———— Scenes from the drama "Chūshingura," etc. ; by Fusatane, Gengyo, Kuniaki, Kunichika, Kunisada (Toyokuni 2nd), Toyokuni, Yoshichika, Yoshitora, and Yoshitoshi. *140 sheets.* (14 × 10).   **O2. A. 1.**

———— Theatrical Scenes ; by Kunichika, Kunisada (Toyokuni 2nd), Toyokuni, Yoshichika, Yoshitoshi, and Yoshitsuru. *216 sheets.* (14 × 10).   **O2. A. 2.**

·———— Portraits of Women with Poems and Views ; by Chikamaro, Chingetsu, Gesshōsai, Gyokuran, Hakuga, Hiroshige, Hokutsui, Isai, Jakushōsai, Kiyoharu, Kiyokuni, Kiyokuni (Torii), Kunihisa, Kunisada (Toyokuni 2nd), Kunisada 2nd, Nanhō, Ōsui, Sadahide, Shigekiyo, Shigemasa, Shōgetsu, Shōshū, Tozan, Tsuruko, Yoshitora, and Yoshitoshi. *82 sheets.* (14½ × 9½).   **O2. A. 3.**

———— Theatrical Scenes, Portraits, etc. ; by Keisai, Kunichika, Kuniteru, Kuniyoshi, Toyokuni, and Yoshichika. *78 sheets.* (14 × 9½).   **O2. A. 4.**

ALBUM—Scenes from the dramas "Chūshingura," and "Sendaihagi," Portraits of Women, etc.; by Kuniyoshi (Ichiyūsai), and Toyokuni. *129 sheets.* (14½ × 10).

O2. A. 5.

——— Portraits of Women, etc.; by Keisai (Yeisen), Kuninao, Kunisada (Toyokuni 2nd), Kuniyasu (Ippōsai), Kuniyoshi (Ichiyūsai), Sadatsuna (Gohōtei), Shigeharu, Tominobu (Kwasentei), Toyokuni, and Yeizan. *119 sheets.* (14½ × 10).

O2. A. 6.

——— Portraits of Women and Theatrical Characters; by Hiroshige, Keisai (Yeisen), Kunisada (Toyokuni 2nd, Kachōrō, Gototei), Kunitomi (Kwasentei), Kuniyasu, Kuniyoshi (Ichiyūsai), Ryūsen, Sadakage (Gokotei), Toyohisa, Toyokuni, and Yeizan. *50 sheets.* (14 × 9½).

O2. A. 7.

——— Amusements of Prince Genji, Theatrical Characters, etc.; by Kunimori, Kunisada (Toyokuni 2nd), Kuniyoshi, and Toyokuni. *21 sheets.* (13¾ × 9¾).

O2. A. 8.

——— Wrestlers, Theatrical Characters, Warriors, etc.; by Hirosada, Keisai (Yeisen), Kunisada (Toyokuni 2nd), Kuniyoshi, Yoshikazu (Ichijusai), Yoshimune (Isshōsai), and Yoshitora (Kinchōrō). *27 sheets.* (14½ × 9¾).

O2. A. 9.

——— Amusements of Prince Genji, Theatrical Scenes, Portraits of Women, etc.; by Keisai (Yeisen), Kunichika, Kunifuke (Isshōsai), Kunimaru (Saikarō), Kunisada (Toyokuni 2nd), Kunisada 2nd, Kuniyasu, Kuniyoshi, Toyokuni, Yoshichika, Yoshikazu (Ichijusai), and Yoshitora. *122 sheets.* (9¾ × 14).

O2. A. 10.

——— Portraits of Women, Theatrical Characters and various Scenes; by Hiroshige (Ichiryūsai), Keisai (Yeisen), Kunichika (Ichiōsai), Kunimasa (Ichijusai), Kunimori (Kochōrō), Kunisada (Toyokuni 2nd, Gototei), Kunitomi (Kwasentei), Kuniyasu (Ippōsai), Kuniyoshi (Ichiyūsai), Sadafusa (Kitchōrō), Shunshō (Kochōyen), Toyokuni, and Yoshitora (Ichimōsai). *60 sheets.* (14¼ × 9½).

O2. A. 11.

ALBUM.—Portraits of Women ; by Daiji, Keisai (Yeisen), Kuniaki, Kunichika, Kunisada (Toyokuni 2nd, Kachōrō), Kunisada 2nd, Kunisato, Kuniteru, Kuniyasu (Ippōsai), Kuniyoshi (Ichiyūsai), Senchō (Teisai), Tominobu (Kwasentei), Toyokuni, Yoshichika (Ikkeisai), Yoshimori, and Yoshitora. *80 sheets.* ($14\frac{1}{4} \times 9\frac{3}{4}$). **O2. A. 12.**

—————— Theatrical Characters, etc. ; by Kunisada (Toyokuni 2nd), Kuniyoshi (Ichiyūsai), and Toyokuni. *100 sheets.* ($14\frac{1}{4} \times 9\frac{3}{4}$). **O2. A. 13.**

—————— Theatrical Scenes ; by Kunisada (Toyokuni 2nd), Kuniyasu, Kuniyoshi, Sadafusa, and Sadahide. *98 sheets, in painted cover.* ($14\frac{1}{2} \times 10$). **O2. A. 14.**

—————— Theatrical Scenes, etc. ; by Hokushū (Shunkōsai), Kunichika, Kunihiko (Kokkisha), Kunikiyo, Kunisada (Toyokuni 2nd, Gototei), Kunisada 2nd, Kuniyoshi (Ichiyūsai), Sadanobu (Hasegawa), Toyokuni, and Yoshikado (Ichirinsai). *80 sheets.* (14×10). **O2. A. 15.**

—————— Portraits of Women, Theatrical Characters, etc. ; by Hiroshige, Kunisada (Toyokuni 2nd), Kunisada 2nd (Baichōrō), Kuniyoshi (Chōōrō), Toyokuni, Yoshitaki, Yoshitora (Kinchōrō),Yoshitsuna (Ittōsai),and Yoshiyuki. *75 sheets.* ($14 \times 9\frac{3}{4}$). **O2. A. 16.**

—————— Theatrical Scenes, Portraits of Women, View of the Fishmarket at Nihombashi, Yedo, etc. ; by Hiroshige, Ichigyokusai, Keisai (Yeisen), Kunichika (Ichiōsai), Kunisada (Toyokuni 2nd, Gototei), Kunisada 2nd (Baichōrō), Kunisato (Ryūsensai), Kuniteru, Kuniyasu, Kuniyoshi, Sadahide (Gyokuran), Sadatora (Gofūtei), Shigenobu (Ichiyūsai). Shunshō (Hōrai), Toyokuni, Yoshifuji (Ippōsai), Yoshikazu (Ichijusai), and Yoshitora (Kinchōrō). *204 sheets.* ($14\frac{1}{4} \times 10$). **O2. A. 17.**

—————— Portraits of Women and Famous Personages, Theatrical and other Scenes, etc. ; by Gengyo, Hiroshige, Keisai (Yeisen), Kunichika, Kunisada (Toyokuni 2nd, Kachōrō), Kunisada 2nd (Baichōrō), Kuniyasu, Kuniyoshi (Chōōrō, Ichiyūsai), Sadatora (Gofūtei), Senchō, Toyokuni, Yeizan, Yoshichika (Ikkeisai), Yoshikazu, and Yoshitsuya (Ichiyeisai). *229 sheets.* (14×10). **O2. A. 18.**

ALBUM.—Azuma Nishikiye. Theatrical Scenes and Characters; by Kuniyoshi (Ichiyūsai), Toyokuni (Ichi-yōsai, Kachōrō), and Yoshichika. *121 sheets.* (14 × 10).
O2. A. 19.

TOYOKUNI.—Album of Theatrical Scenes. *410 sheets.* 5 vols. (13¾ × 9¾).
O2. A. 20.

ALBUM.—Portraits of Women, Theatrical Characters, Illustrations of the Silkworm Industry, etc.; by Keisai (Yeisen), Kunichika, Kunimasa (Ichijusai, Baidō), Kunisada (Toyokuni 2nd, Kachōrō), Kunisada 2nd, (Baichōrō), Kuniyoshi (Ichiyūsai), Ōsai, Toyokuni, Yoshichika (Chōkarō, Ikkeisai), and Yoshifuji (Ippōsai). *40 sheets* (14 × 9¾).
O2. A. 21.

———— Theatrical Scenes and Portraits, Caricatures, etc.; by Hiroshige, Kuniyoshi, Sadashige, Toyokuni, Yoshifuji, Yoshitora, and Yoshitsuya. *46 sheets.* (14¼ × 9¾).
O2. A. 22.

——— Theatrical Scenes, Portraits, etc.; by Keisai, Kunisada (Toyokuni 2nd), Kuniyoshi, Sadafusa, Yoshimune, and Yoshitsuya. *42 sheets.* (14 × 10).
O2. A. 23.

.——— Theatrical and Humorous Characters; by Kuniyoshi, Tori-jo (*female artist*), and Toyokuni. *89 sheets.* (14¼ × 9¼).
O2. A. 24.

——— Theatrical Characters, Picture of the Seven Gods of Good Fortune humorously drawn, etc.; by Baiso (Gengyo), Chikuyōdō, Fujimaru, Fusatane, Gokyōtei, Hiroshige, Ichi-ō, Kiku-jo (*female artist*), Kuniaki, Kunichika, Kunisada (Toyokuni 2nd), Kwakuju (Meirindō, *female artist*), Rigyoku, Yoshichika (Ikkeisai), Yoshimori, Yoshitora, Yoshitoshi (Ikkwaisai) and Yoshitsuya (Ichiyeisai). *104 sheets.* (14 × 9½).
O2. A. 25.

——— Portraits of Women and various Humorous and other Scenes; by Hirosada, Hiroshige, Hokuchō (Shunshosai), Keisai (Yeisen), Kunichika, Kuniharu, Kunisada (Toyokuni 2nd), Kunisada 2nd (Baichōrō), Kuniteru, Kuniyoshi, Shigeharu (Gyokuryūtei), Shigenobu, Toyokuni, Tsukimaro (Bokutei), Yoshichika, and Yoshikazu (Ichijusai). *101 sheets.* (14¼ × 9¾).
O2. A. 26.

ALBUM.—Scenes from the Drama "Chūshingura" (the Story of the Forty-seven Rōnin), Views of noted places in Yedo, etc.; by Hiroshige, Keisai (Yeisen), Kunimaru, Kuninao, Kunitsuna, Shigenobu (Ichiyūsai), and Toyokuni. *88 sheets.* (9½ × 14). **O2. A. 27.**

——— Theatrical Scenes : by Ashiyuki (Kegyokudō), Hokuchō (Shunshosai), Hokushū (Shunkōsai), Hokuyei (Shunkōsai), Kunihiro, Kunisada (Toyokuni 2nd), Sadamasu (Gochōtei), Sadanobu, Shigeharu (Gyokuryūtei), and Yoshikuni (Jukōdō). *22 sheets.* (14½ × 9½). **O2. B. 1.**

——— Portraits of Women, and Theatrical Characters ; by Shūchō (Tamagawa), Shuntei, Toyokuni, Utamaro, Yeishi, and Yeizan. *29 sheets.* (14¼ × 10¼). **O2. B. 2.**

——— Portraits of Women in various Scenes, and Theatrical Characters ; by Hiroshige, Keisai (Yeisen), Kunimasa, Kunisada (Toyokuni 2nd, Kachōrō, Gototei), Sadahide (Gyokuransai), and Toyokuni. *32 sheets.* (14 × 10). **O2. B. 3.**

——— Theatrical Scenes; by Ashiyuki (Kegwadō), Hokuchō (Shunshosai), Hokumyō (Shunkōsai), Hokusei (Hokkai, Shunshisai), Hokushū (Shunkōsai), Hokuyei (Shunkōsai), Kunihiro, Masakuni (Jukwakudō), Shigefusa, Shigeharu (Gyokuryūtei), Shunkō, Tamikuni (Jiryūsai, Kōgwadō), Toyokuni, Umekuni (Jukyōdō), and Yoshikuni (Jukōdō). *83 sheets.* (14¾ × 10¼). **O2. B. 4.**

——— Theatrical Scenes : by Kuniaki, Kunichika, Kunisada (Toyokuni 2nd), Toyokuni, and Yoshichika. *125 sheets.* (14½ × 10). **O2. B. 5.**

——— Theatrical Scenes and Characters, by Keisai (Yeisen), Kuniaki, Kunisada (Toyokuni 2nd), Sadafusa, Toyokuni, and Yoshifuji. *59 sheets.* (14¼ × 10). **O2. B. 6.**

——— Theatrical Characters : by Kiyonaga, Kunihisa, Kunimasa, Kunimitsu, Shunki, Shunyei, and Toyokuni. *74 sheets.* (14¾ × 9¾). **O2. B. 7.**

Broken Up.

02. A. 27.   Transferred to print collection

Broken Up.

02. B. 7.   Transferred to Catalogue, pa
            J 4941 - 5014.

ALBUM.—Portraits of Women, Theatrical Characters, etc.; by Hiroshige, Keisai (Yeisen), Kunisada (Toyokuni 2nd, Gototei, Kachōrō), Kunisada 2nd (Ichijusai), Kuniyasu (Ippōsai), Kuniyoshi (Ichiyūsai), Sadahide (Gountei), Sadakage (Gokotei), Senchō (Teisai), Tominobu (Kwasentei), Toyokuni, Yeizan, and Yoshitora (Kinchōrō). *100 sheets.* (14½ × 10). **O2. B. 8.**

———— Theatrical Characters, etc.; by Hirokuni, Hirosada, Kunisada (Toyokuni 2nd, Ichiyōsai), Kuniyoshi, Sadamasu, Sadanobu, and Toyokuni. *58 sheets.* (13¾ × 9¾). **O2. B. 9.**

———— Theatrical Scenes and Characters; by Kunisada (Toyokuni 2nd, Kachōrō, Ichiyōsai), Kunisada 2nd (Baichōrō), Kuniteru, Kuniyoshi (Ichiyūsai, Chōōrō,) and Toyokuni. *30 sheets.* (14¼ × 10). **O2. B. 10.**

———— Portraits of Women, Theatrical Scenes, one of the Eight celebrated Views of Lake Biwa, etc.; by Keisai (Yeisen), Kunisada (Toyokuni 2nd, Gototei, Kachōrō), Kuniyasu (Ippōsai), Kuniyoshi (Ichiyūsai), Sadafusa (Gokitei), Sadahide (Gountei), Sadatora (Gofūtei), Sadatsuna (Gohōtei), Tominobu (Kwasentei), Toyokuni (Gosotei), and Yoshishige (Ichiyōsai). *118 sheets.* (14¾ × 10½). **O2. B. 11.**

———— Portraits of Women; by Keisai (Yeisen), Kunimaru, Kunisada (Toyokuni 2nd, Gototei), Kuniyoshi, Tominobu (Kwasentei), Toyokuni, Utamaro, and Yeizan. *32 sheets.* (14¼ × 10). **O2. B. 12.**

————Portraits of Women; by Keisai (Yeisen), Kunisada (Toyokuni 2nd, Gototei), Kuniyasu, Kuniyoshi (Ichiyūsai), Sadafusa (Gokitei), and Sadakage (Gokotei). *38 sheets.* (14¾ × 10). **O2. B. 13.**

———— Portraits of Women; by Keisai (Yeisen), Kuniaki, Kunichika, Kunihiro, Kunihisa, Kunikazu, Kunikiyo, Kunimaro, Kunisada (Toyokuni 2nd, Kachōrō), Kunisato, Kunishige, Kunitomo, Kuniyasu, Kuniyoshi (Ichiyūsai), Sadafusa (Gokitei), Sadatora (Gofūtei), Toyokuni, Yeizan, and Yoshitora (Kinchōrō). *88 sheets.* (14½ × 10). **O2. B. 14.**

————Theatrical Scenes, etc.; by Ashihiro, Ashikiyo, Ashitsura, Ashiyuki, Hokushū (Shunkōsai), Hokuyei (Shumbaisai), Kunihiro, Kunisada (Toyokuni 2nd, Kachōrō, Ichiyōsai), Kuniteru (Issensai), Kuniyoshi (Ichiyūsai), Shigeharu (Gyokuryūtei), Shunchō, Shunkō, Shuntei, and Yoshikuni (Jukōdō). *62 sheets.* (14¾ × 10). **O2. B. 15.**

ALBUM.—Theatrical Scenes and Characters, etc.; by Kuniyoshi, and Toyokuni. *35 sheets.* (14½ × 10). **O2. B. 16.**

———— Theatrical Scenes, and studies of Dancing; by Kuniaki, Kunichika, Kunisada (Toyokuni 2nd), Kunisada 2nd, and Toyokuni. *45 sheets.* (14½ × 10). **O2. B. 17.**

———— Theatrical and Battle Scenes, Portraits of Women, etc.; by Hiroshige, Kunisada (Toyokuni 2nd), Kuniyoshi, Sadahide, Yoshifuji, Yoshitora, and Yoshitsuna. *57 sheets.* (14½ × 10). **O2. B. 18.**

———— Theatrical Scenes; by Kunisada (Toyokuni 2nd), Kuniyasu, Sadafusa, and Toyokuni. *53 sheets.* (15 × 10¼). **O2. B. 19.**

————Theatrical Scenes; by Kunisada (Toyokuni 2nd), and Kuniyoshi. *46 sheets.* (14¾ × 10). **O2. B. 20.**

————Portraits of Women; by Keisai (Yeisen), Kunisada (Toyokuni 2nd, Gototei), Kunitomi (Kwasentei), Kuniyasu (Ippōsai), Kuniyoshi (Ichiyūsai), Tominobu (Kwasentei), Toyokuni, Utamaro, Yeishi, Yeishin, and Yeizan. *40 sheets.* (14¾ × 10¼). **O2. B. 21.**

———— Portraits of Women and Theatrical Scenes; by Keisai (Yeisen), Kunihiro, Kunihisa (*female artist*), Kuninao, Kunisada (Toyokuni 2nd, Kachōrō), Kuniyoshi (Ichiyūsai), Sadafusa (Gokitei), Senchō (Teisai), Shunshō (Hōrai), and Toyokuni. *72 sheets.* (14½ × 10). **O2. B. 22.**

————Theatrical Scenes, Warriors, etc.; by Fusatane, Gakutei, Harusada, Hirokage, Hirokuni, Hirosada, Hiroshige, Keisai (Yeisen), Kunikazu, Kunisada (Toyokuni 2nd, Kachōrō, Kokuteisha, Ichiyōsai), Kuniyasu, Kuniyoshi (Ichiyūsai), Minehiro, Moriyoshi, Sadahiro, Sadanobu (Kinkwadō), Sadayoshi, Shigenobu, Shungyoku, Shunsui, Shunyei, Toyokuni, Yoshichika, Yoshikazu (Ichijusai), Yoshitaki, Yoshitora (Kinchōrō), and Yoshitoyo. *123 sheets.* (14½ × 10.) **O2. B. 23.**

———— — Theatrical Characters, Portraits of Women, etc.; by Ashihiro, Hokuju (Shunshosai), Hokumyō (Sekkōtei), Hokuyei (Shumbaisai), Kunihiro, Kunisada (Toyokuni 2nd, Gototei), Kuniyoshi (Ichiyūsai), Sadahiro (Gorakutei), Sadamasa, Sadamasu (Gochōtei), Sadanobu, Sadatsugu (Gochōtei), and Sadayoshi. *119 sheets.* (14¾ × 10). **O2. B. 24.**

Broken Up.

01.C.33 No 44. contains an earlier print of No 1 in this
album by Sadahiro: see note on P.17.

/ Shigeharu

ALBUM.—Theatrical Characters; by Hokuyei (Shumbaisai), Kunihiro (Gwanjōsai), Kunitsuru (Utagawa), Nobuharu (Hasegawa), Sadaharu (Hasegawa), ~~Sadaharu~~ (Ryūsai), Sadahiro (Utagawa), Sadamasu (Gochōtei), Sadanobu (Hasegawa), Sadayoshi (Utagawa), and Yoshitsugu. *103 sheets..* (14¾ × 10).　　　　　**O2. B. 25.**

—————— Yakusha Yedehon. Pictures of Theatrical Performances; by Kuniyoshi (Ichiyūsai), Sadashige (Ichiyūsai), Shigemitsu, Toyokuni (Ichiyōsai, Kachōrō), and Yoshifuji (Ippōsai). *129 sheets.* (14¾ × 9¾).　**O2. B. 26.**

——————Theatrical Portraits, Humorous and other Scenes, etc.; by Hirokage, Hiroshige, Kunisada (Toyokuni 2nd, Ichiyōsai, Kachōrō, Ki-ō, Kokuteisha,) Kuniyoshi (Ichiyūsai), Toyokuni (Ichiyōsai, Kachōrō), and Yoshitsuya (Ichiyeisai). *139 sheets.* (14½ × 9½).　**O2. B. 27.**

—————— Theatrical and other Scenes, Humorous Pictures, etc.; by Kuniyoshi, Toyokuni, Yoshichika, and Yoshitora. *30 sheets.* (14¾ × 10).　　　　**O2. B. 28.**

—————— Theatrical Scenes, etc.; by Kuniyoshi, Shōjō Kyōsai, and Toyokuni. *30 sheets.* (14½ × 10).　　**O2. B. 29.**

—————— Portraits of Theatrical and other Characters, Various Scenes, etc.; by Chikamaro (Shōjō), Hiroshige (Ichiryūsai), Kunisada 2nd (Baichōrō), Kuniyoshi, Toyokuni, Yoshichika (Ikkeisai), and Yoshitsuya (Ichiyeisai), *141 sheets.* (14½ × 9½).　　　**O2. B. 30.**

—————— Pictures of Beautiful Women, some with quotations from the Hundred Poems, Scenes of the Tamagawa in six different provinces, Theatrical Characters, etc.; by Kunisada (Toyokuni 2nd, Kachōrō, Ichiyōsai, Gototei), Kuniyoshi (Ichiyūsai), and Yoshichika. *76 sheets.* (14½ × 10).　　　　　**O2. B. 31.**

—————— Theatrical and other Scenes, Portraits of Actors, a View of Yenoshima, etc.; by Hiroshige, Kunisada (Toyokuni 2nd), Kuniyoshi, and Yoshifuji. *56 sheets.* (14¾ × 10).　　　　　**O2. B. 32.**

—————— Portraits of Women, Theatrical Characters and Warriors; by Keisai (Yeisen), Kunisada (Toyokuni 2nd), Kuniyasu, Kuniyoshi, and Toyokuni. *26 sheets* (14½ × 10¼).　　　　　**O2. B. 33.**

ALBUM.—Theatrical Scenes; Portraits of Women, Famous Personages, etc., by Kuniyoshi, and Toyokuni. *118 sheets.* (14½ × 10). **O2. B. 34.**

——— Theatrical Characters; by Hokuyei (Shumbaisai), Kunihiro, Kunisada (Toyokuni 2nd, Gototei), Kunitsuru, Kuniyoshi (Ichiyūsai), Sadanobu (Hasegawa), Shigeharu (Ryūsai), and Toyokuni. *84 sheets.* (14½ × 10). **O2. C. 2.**

——— Portraits of Women, Theatrical Characters, etc.; by Hiroshige, Keisai (Yeisen), Kunichika (Ichiōsai), Kunihiko (Kokkisha), Kunimasa (Ichijusai), Kunisada (Toyokuni 2nd, Kachōrō, Ichiyōsai), Kunisada 2nd (Baichōrō), Kunisato, Kuniyoshi (Chōōrō, Ichiyūsai), Kwachōrō, Teisai, Toyokuni, Yoshifuji (Ippōsai), Yoshiharu, Yoshikazu (Ichijusai), and Yoshitora (Ichimōsai). *100 sheets.* (14 × 10). **O2. C. 3.**

——— Portraits of Women and Theatrical Characters; by Hiroshige, Hōgyoku (*female artist*), Keisai (Yeisen), Kunisada (Toyokuni 2nd, Kachōrō, Ichiyōsai, Gototei), Kunisada 2nd (Ichijusai), Kuniyasu, Kuniyoshi (Ichiyūsai, Chōōrō), Ōsai, Sadahide (Gyokuransai), Sadakage (Gokotei), Sadatora (Gofūtei), Seisai (Yeiichi), Senchō (Sogetsuyen, Teisai), Shunshō (Hōrai, Kochōyen), Toyokuni (Gosotei), Yeizan, Yoshichika (Chōkarō), Yoshifuji, Yoshikazu (Ichijusai), and Yoshitora (Kinchōrō). *100 sheets.* (14½ × 10.) **O2. C. 4.**

——— Portraits of Women; by Fusatane, Hiroshige, Keisai (Yeisen), Kunichika, Kunisada (Toyokuni 2nd, Kachōrō, Ichiyōsai, Gototei), Kunisada 2nd (Baichōrō, Ichijusai), Kuniteru (Ichiyūsai), Kuniyasu, Kuniyoshi (Ichiyūsai, Chōōrō), Sadakage (Gokotei), Sadashige (Utagawa), Sadatora (Gofūtei), Senchō (Teisai), Toyokuni (Ichiyōsai), Yoshifuji (Ippōsai), Yoshikazu (Ichikawa), and Yoshitora. *100 sheets.* (14 × 10). **O2. C. 5.**

——— Portraits of Women, some with appropriate quotations from the "Hundred Poems"; by Hiroshige, Keisai (Yeisen, Ippitsuan), Kunimasa, Kunisada (Toyokuni 2nd, Kachōrō, Gototei, Kokuteisha, Ichiyōsai), Kuniyasu (Ippōsai), Sadahide (Gountei), Sadatora (Gofūtei), Senchō (Teisai), Toyokuni (Gosotei), Yeizan, and Yoshitora (Kinchōrō). *100 sheets.* (13¾ × 9¾). **O2. C. 6.**

ALBUM.—Portraits of Women, Theatrical Characters, etc.; by Keisai (Yeisen), Kunichika, Kunimaru (Ichiyensai), Kunimori (Kachōrō), Kunisada (Toyokuni 2nd, Kachōrō, Gototei), Kunisada 2nd (Baichōrō), Kuniyasu, Kuniyoshi (Ichiyūsai, Chōōrō), Sadafusa (Gokitei), Sadahide (Gyokuransai), Sadakage (Gokotei), Sadatora (Gofūtei), Shigenobu (Ichiyūsai), Shōjūsai, Shunshō (Kochōyen), Toyokuni (Ichiyōsai), Yoshichika (Ikkeisai), Yoshikazu (Ichijusai), Yoshitora (Kinchōrō), and Yoshitsuya (Ichiyeisai). *102 sheets.* (14 × 9¾). **O2. C. 7.**

—— Portraits of Women, Theatrical Characters, etc.; by Hiroshige, Keisai (Yeisen, Ippitsuan), Kunichika, Kunisada (Toyokuni 2nd, Gototei, Kachōrō, Ichiyōsai), Kunisada 2nd (Ichijusai, Baichōrō), Kunisato, Kuniteru, Kuniyasu, Kuniyoshi (Ichiyūsai, Chōōrō), Sadahide (Gyokurantei), Sadakage (Gokotei), Sadatora (Gofūtei), Shigenobu, Shunshō (Kochōyen), Toyokuni (Gosotei), Yeizan, Yoshikazu (Ichijusai), Yoshishige (Ichiyōsai), and Yoshitora. *100 sheets.* (14½ × 9¾). **O2. C. 8.**

—— Portraits of Women, and a View of Kyōto; by Hiroshige, Ichigyokusai, Keisai (Yeisen), Kunimaru (Saikarō), Kunisada (Toyokuni 2nd, Gototei, Kachōrō, Ichiyōsai), Kunisada 2nd, Kunitomi (Kwasentei), Kuniyoshi (Chōōrō, Ichiyūsai), Kuniyoshi (Isshō), Sadahide (Gyokuran), Shigenobu, Toyokuni, Yeizan (Kikugawa), Yoshichika (Ikkeisai), Yoshifuji (Ippōsai), Yoshikazu (Ichijusai), and Yoshitora (Ichimōsai, Kinchōrō). *98 sheets* (14½ × 10). **O2. C. 9.**

—— Portraits of Women, and Landscapes; by Gokotei, Hiroshige (Ichiryūsai), Keisai (Yeisen), Kunimaru (Ichiyensai), Kuninao, Kunisada (Toyokuni 2nd, Kachōrō, Gototei, Ki-ō), Kunitomi (Kwasentei), Kuniyasu, Kuniyoshi (Ichiyūsai), Sadafusa (Gokitei), Sadahide, Sadatora (Gofūtei), Senchō (Teisai), Shigenobu, Yeizan (Kikugawa), Yoshifuji (Ippōsai), and Yoshitora (Ichimōsai). *100 sheets.* (14 × 9½). **O2. C. 10.**

—— Theatrical Scenes, a View of Miyagawa in Ise, etc.; by Ashiyuki (Kegwadō), Fujimaru (Yanagijima), Hiroshige, Hokushū (Shunkōsai), Hokuyei (Shumbasai, Shunkōsai), Kunichika (Ichiōsai), Kunihiro, Kunisada (Toyokuni 2nd, Gototei, Kachōrō, Ki-ō),

Kunisada 2nd (Baichōrō), Kuniyasu, Kuniyoshi (Ichiyūsai), Sadanobu (Hasegawa), Sadayuki, Shigeharu (Ryūsai, Gyokuryūtei), Toyokuni (Ichiyōsai), Yoshichika, Yoshikuni, and Yoshitora. *100 sheets.* $(13\frac{1}{2} \times 9\frac{1}{2})$.

O2. D. 1.

ALBUM.—Portraits of Women, and Theatrical Characters; by Hiroshige, Keisai (Yeisen), Kunichika, Kunimori (Ippōsai), Kunisada (Toyokuni 2nd), Kunisada 2nd, Kuniteru (Ichiyūsai), Kuniyoshi, Sadatora (Gofūtei), Senchō (Teisai), Shigenobu, Toyokuni, Yoshichika (Ikkeisai), Yoshikazu (Ichijusai), and Yoshitoshi (Kwaisai). *100 sheets.* $(13\frac{1}{2} \times 9\frac{1}{2})$.

O2. D. 2.

——— Portraits of Women, and Theatrical Characters; by Hiroshige, Keisai (Yeisen), Kuniaki, Kunimasa (Ichijusai), Kunisada (Toyokuni 2nd, Ichiyōsai, Kachōrō), Kunisada 2nd (Kunimasa, Ichijusai), Kuniteru (Sadashige), Kuniyoshi (Chōōrō, Ichiyūsai), Sadahide (Gyokuransai), Shigenobu (Ichiyūsai), Toyokuni, and Yoshitora. *100 sheets.* $(13\frac{1}{2} \times 9\frac{1}{2})$.

O2. D. 3.

——— Portraits of Women; by Keisai (Yeisen), Kunimori (Kochōyen, *pupil of* Toyokuni), Kunisada (Toyokuni 2nd, Kachōrō, Ichiyōsai, Gototei), Kunisato, Kunitora, Kuniyasu (Ippōsai), Kuniyoshi (Ichiyūsai, Chōōrō), Kwachōrō (Utagawa), Sadafusa (Gokitei), Sadahide (Gyokuransai, Utagawa), Sadakoma, Shigenobu, Yeizan (Kikugawa), Yoshichika (Ikkeisai), Yoshifuji (Ippōsai), Yoshifusa (Ippōsai), Yoshikazu (Ichijusai), Yoshimori (Ikkwōsai), Yoshimune (Isshōsai), and Yoshitora (Ichimōsai, Kinchōrō). *100 sheets.* $(13\frac{1}{2} \times 9\frac{1}{2})$.

O2. D. 4.

——— Portraits of Women, Theatrical Characters from "Sendaihagi," and various Scenes; by Hiroshige, Ichigyokusai, Kunichika, Kunikane, Kunisada (Toyokuni 2nd, Kachōrō), Kuniteru (Ichiyūsai), Kuniyasu, Kuniyoshi (Ichiyūsai), Toyokuni, and Yoshiharu (Ichibaisai). *132 sheets.* $(13\frac{1}{2} \times 9\frac{1}{2})$.

O2. D. 5.

——— Theatrical Scenes; by Hokuchō (Shunshosai), Hokumyō (Sekkōtei), Hokuyei (Shumbaisai), Kunimaru, Kunisada (Toyokuni 2nd, Gototei), Kuniyasu, Kuniyoshi (Ichiyūsai), Sadayoshi (Utagawa), Shunshi (Gwatoken), Toyokuni, Usai, and Yoshimune (Shōsai). *100 sheets.* $(14 \times 9\frac{3}{4})$.

O2. D. 6.

ALBUM.—Portraits of Women; by Hiroshige,Keisai (Yeisen), Kunikane, Kunimori (Ippōsai, Kochōyen, Shunshō), Kunisada (Toyokuni 2nd, Gototei, Kachōrō, Ichiyōsai), Kuniteru (Ichiyūsai), Kunitsuna (Ichirantei), Kuniyasu, Kuniyoshi (Ichiyūsai, Chōōrō), Kwachōrō, Sadafusa (Gokitei, Kitchōrō), Sadahide (Gyokuransai), Shigenobu, Tominobu (Kwasentei), Toyokuni, Yeizan, Yoshifuji (Ippōsai), Yoshikazu (Ichijusai), and Yoshitora (Kinchōrō, Ichimōsai). *100 sheets.* (13½ × 9¼). **O2. D. 7.**

———— Portraits of Women and Theatrical Characters ; by Hiroshige (Ichiryūsai), Keisai (Yeisen), Kunisada (Toyokuni 2nd, Kachōrō), Kunisada 2nd (Baichōrō), Kunisato (Ryūsensai), Kunitomi (Kwasentei), Kunitora, Kunitsuna (Ichiransai), Kuniyasu (Ippōsai), Kuniyoshi (Ichiyūsai, Chōōrō), Morinobu (Kochōyen), Sadahide (Gountei), Senchō (Teisai), Shigenobu (Ichiyūsai), Tominobu (Kwasentei), Toyokuni (Gosotei), Yoshifuji (Ippōsai), Yoshikazu (Ichijusai), Yoshikoma (Ichijusai), Yoshimori (Ikkwōsai), Yoshitora (Kinchōrō, Ichimōsai), and Yoshitsuya (Ichiyeisai). *100 sheets.* (13¼ × 9½).
O2. D. 8.

———— Theatrical Characters, Portraits of Women, and various Scenes ; by Hiroshige (Ichiryūsai), Kunichika, Kunihiko, Kunihisa, Kunisada (Toyokuni 2nd, Kachōrō, Ichiyōsai), Kunisada 2nd (Baichōrō, Ichijusai), Kuniteru, Kuniyo-hi (Ichiyūsai, Chōōrō), Sadahide (Gountei), Toyokuni, Yoshichika (Ikkeisai), Yoshikado (Ichirinsai), Yoshikazu (Ichijusai), and Yoshimori. *100 sheets.* (14 × 10). **O2. D. 9.**

———— Portraits of Women ; by Kunisada (Toyokuni 2nd, Gototei), and Kuniyoshi (Chōōrō). *30 sheets.* (15¼ × 10¼). **O2. D. 10.**

———— Theatrical Scenes, including two from the drama "Chūshingura," (the Story of Forty-seven Rōnin) ; by Ashiyuki (Kegwadō), Hirosada, Hokuchō (Shunshosai), Kuniharu, Kunihiro, Kunisada (Toyokuni 2nd, Gototei, Kachōrō, Ichiyōsai, Ki-ō), Kunitomi (Kwasentei), Kuniyasu (Ippōsai), Kuniyoshi (Ichiyūsai), Shigeharu (Gyokuryūtei), and Yoshimaru (*pupil of* Kuniyoshi, *age 14*). *94 sheets.* (13½ × 9½). **O2. D. 11.**

ALBUM.—Portraits of Women ; by Hiroshige, Keisai (Yeisen), Kunisada (Toyokuni 2nd), Kuniyasu, Yeishin (Tenshūsai), Yeishun (Senchōsai), and Yeizan (Kikugawa). *60 sheets.* (13½ × 9). **O2. D. 12.**

———— Portraits of Women ; by Keisai (Yeisen), Kunisada (Toyokuni 2nd, Gototei, Kachōrō), Kunitomi (Kwa sentei), Kuniyasu (Ippōsai), Sadatora (Gofūtei), Shunsen, Toyokuni, Yeishin (Kikugawa, Tenshūsai), and Yeizan (Kikugawa). *60 sheets.* (14 × 9½). **O2. D. 13.**

———— Portraits of Women ; by Keisai (Yeisen), Kunikane, Kunimune, Kunisada (Toyokuni 2nd, Kachōrō, Gototei), Kuniyasu, Kuniyoshi (Ichiyūsai), Shunkō (Shunsen), Shunsen, Shunshō (Kochōyen), Toyokuni (Gosotei), Yeishin (Kikugawa), and Yeizan (Kikugawa). *60 sheets.* (13¾ × 9). **O2. D. 14.**

———— Theatrical Scenes; by Hironobu, Hirosada, Sadahiro, Sadakatsu, Sadayoshi, Toyokuni, and Yoshitaki. *30 sheets.* (10 × 7). **O3. F. 13.**

———— Portraits of Women, Theatrical Scenes, Views, etc. ; by Hiroshige, Kunisada (Toyokuni 2nd), Kunisada 2nd, Kuniyoshi, Toyokuni, and Yoshifuji. *69 sheets.* (10 × 12¾). **O4. F. 6.**

———— Portraits of Women ; by Hiroshige, Keisai (Yeisen), Kunimori (Ippōsai), Kunisada (Toyokuni 2nd, Kachōrō), Kunisato, Kuniyasu, Sadahide, Senchō (Teisai), Tominobu (Kwasentei), Yeizan, Yoshikazu (Ichijusai), and Yoshitora (Ichimōsai). *66 sheets.* (12¾ × 9). **O4. F. 7.**

———— Portraits of Women ; by Keisai (Yeisen), Kunimori (Ippōsai, Kochōyen), Kunisada (Toyokuni 2nd, Gototei), Kunitomi (Kwasentei), Sadafusa (Gokitei), and Shunkō (Shunsen). *32 sheets.* (13 × 9). **O4. F. 8.**

———— Portraits of Women ; by Keisai (Yeisen), Shunsen, and Yeizan. *24 sheets.* (13 × 9). **O4. F. 9.**

———— Theatrical Scenes, Portraits of famous personages, etc. ; by Hironobu, Kunikazu (Kwayōrō), Kuniyoshi, Munehiro, Sadahiro (Shōkwōtci), Sadanobu, Shōshin, Yoshichika (Ikkeisai), Yoshiharu, Yoshikazu (Ichijusai), Yoshimori (Ikkwōsai), Yoshitaki (Ichiyōtei), and Yoshitora. *101 sheets.* (13½ × 9½). **O4. F. 10.**

———— Portraits of Women ; by Hidemaro, Keisai (Yeisen), Kuniyasu, Senchō (Teisai), Shigemasa, and Yeizan. *28 sheets.* (13¾ × 9½). **O4. F. 11.**

bvrken Mg.

Broken Up.

Yoshimaro.

Broken Up.

ALBUM.—Portraits of Women; by Hidemaro, Kanamaro, Masaatsu (Kitagawa), Ryūkoku, Toyokuni, Tsukimaro, Utamaro, and Yeizan. *30 sheets.* (12 × 8). **O5. A. 10.**

——— Portraits of Women; by Bunkyō (Sakuragawa), Shikō, Shunchō, Toyokuni, Utamaro, and Yeishi. *24 sheets.* (12 × 9). **O5. A. 11.**

——— Theatrical Scenes, Carved Figures by Hidari Jingorō, and a copy of Caricatures on a Wall; by Kuniyoshi (Ichiyūsai), and Toyokuni. *42 sheets (in 3 portions).* (14½ × 9¾). **O5. C. 20.**

——— Theatrical Scenes by Kunikazu, Shōshin, Yoshitaka, and Yoshitaki. *38 sheets.* (9¾ × 7). **O5. C. 21.**

——— Portraits of Theatrical Characters; by Hirokuni, Hirosada, Kiyosada, Kunimasu (Ichijutei), Kunishige, Munehiro, Sadahiro, Sadamasu, and Sadanobu. *70 sheets.* (10 × 7). **O5. C. 22.**

INDEX OF NAMES OF AUTHORS
AND ARTISTS.

Adzuma Kenzaburō. 19

Akashi, Chūshichi. 11
Akisato Ritō. 34
Andō, See Yenshi.
Aoki, see Nanboku.

Araki, See Kwampo

Beisai. 56.
Beisen, see Kubota Beisen.

Bunchō, Tani. 15

Bunzan, see Higuchi.
Chiharu, Takashima. 22.

Chihaya Jōchō. 19.

Chubei, Nonomura. 44.

Chuka, Nakamura. 84.

Chūshichi; see Akashi.

Fujihoko, Senzaiyen. 11.

Fuko, See Matsumoto.

Giokuden, Ishida. 29.

Gotō Tokujirō, See Tokujirō

Hōitsu. 9, 17.

Hokkyo, see Nunzen.

Hokio, See Shumboku

Hanabusa, see Itchō

Hayato, see Ōoka

Hokusai. 1760 - 1849.

Hidenobu, Tosa. 15

Higuchi, Bunzan. 12

Hikohichi, Matsudaya. 44

Homma Yoichi. 42

Hori, see Kisaburo

Hotta, see Renzan.

Hōyen. 38.

Hiroshige. 1797 - 1858. 47

Rōnin, 02. A. 27.

Katsugawa, see Shunsho.
Kawanabe, see Kiōsai.

Keinen, Imao. 9
Kashū, Numado. 9
Katsushika Club. 8
~~Keisai (? Ikkeisai).~~ 9   Kōboyashi, see Yeitaku.
Keisai, Ippitsuan, Yeisen. 17.
Keisai, Kitao. 13   Kodama, see Naganari.
                     Koheiji. Ichiba.
Keisai, Yeisen. 17. Kōgetsudō.
                     Kojiki.
                     Kohitsu. see Ryoi.
                     Kondo. Morishige.

Ken-ichirō, see Nishiyama. Kimura Tokutaro.
Kenzaburō, see Adzuma.
                          * Korusai. (Harunobu)

Kidshigorō, Mori. 60
Kichurobei, see Yamawaka.
Kikuchi, see Yōsai.   Kinsen, Sudzuki.
Kikurō, see Tanaka.
Kimura, Tokutaro. 15   Kinsuke, see Sugita.
Kihei, Kikuya. 44
Kinsuke, see Sugita.   Kōseidō, Nakazawa.
Kikuya. see Kihei.
Kiōsai, Kawanabe Tōyuku. 13 Kubota Beisen. 22

Kiōsai, Shōjō. 64
Kiōsai, Kawanabe 30.9.
Kisaburo, Hori. 14   Kumasaka, see Ransai.
Kitagawa. see Utamaro.
Kitao. see Masanobu.
Kitao, Masayoshi † 1824.
       called also Djoshin. see Kuniyoshi.
Kitao, Shigemasa. 1739-1819.
Kitoo, see.

Samba, Shikitei   30, 59.

Sanjin, _see_ Sugakudō.

Sasaya, Singorō.   44.

Sawaki, _see_ Yoshimosuke.

Seitei, ~~see~~ Watanabe " ~~Seitei~~

Senzaiyen, _see_ Fujihoko

Shiben, _see_ Matsuoka.

Suwara . 18

Sunen, Minamoto . 16

Tachibana , see Minko

Tachibana,, Hochiyo . 28

Taguchi, see Tomoki .   Tohiro † 1728 . see 01.8.

Takai , Ranzan . 28.

Takase, see Tomohiro .   Toyokuni . 1769-1825 .
Takashima , see Chihara .   Toyokuni I . Utagawa .
Tadakichi , Yebishiya . 44
Taki . see Kwatei .

Tanaka , Jirokichi . 9.

Tanaka , Kikuo . 18

                Toyuku, see Kiōsai

Tani , see Bunchō   Tesai . = Hokuba .
Tanyu . Kanō . 15.   Tesai . = ~~see kiosai~~ .
Teika . 29.

                Tsushō .

                Tsuyonage .

Tokei , see Niwa .

Tokujirō , Gotō . 11-40.   Uruu, see Masakaz

Tokutaro , see Kimura

                Useki . Ozaki .

Tomekichi , Yegawa . 22.

Tomohiro , Takase . 22.

Tomoki , Taguchi . 18.

Tosa , see Hidenobu .

Toseiken . 44.

<u>Hiroshige</u>.	02. A. 7.
Keisai Yeisen.	02. A. 7.
Kunisada.	02. A. 7.
Yeizan.	02. A. 7.
Yūbi – Kazan, <u>see</u> Shūjin.	
Foto Toyohisa.	02. A. 7.
Kunitome.	02. A. 7.
Riūsen.	02. A. 7. & 02. A. 11/27 same subject by Kunisada.

Blue Prints
02 B. 11. Kuniyoshi. J 2831 etc.
3203. Women making engravings.

www.ingramcontent.com/pod-product-compliance
Lightning Source LLC
Chambersburg PA
CBHW030837270326
41928CB00007B/1103